PERSONALITY

AND

PREJUDICE

Personality and Prejudice

EDUCATIONAL DISCRIMINATION
OF THE INTROVERTED
INDEPENDENT THINKER

William K. Lawrence, Ed.D.

Paramount Education

Washington D.C.

This book consists of previously reported educational primary and secondary research. Original parts of the research design and pre-existing data have been omitted from this edition for the sake of space and readability. The results and opinions are not a representation of any of the associated institutions. This book is also not a representation of any of the sources, scholars, or theorists. The author bares sole responsibility for the research and expressed conclusions.

Paramount Education,
P.O. Box 1150
Washington D.C. 20009

A cooperative approach to the humanities and social sciences through education, research, and writing.

Copyright © 2016 William K. Lawrence

Author Photo: Julie Lawrence

All rights reserved. No part of this book may be reproduced in any form or by any electronic or mechanical means without written permission from the author, except by a reviewer or researcher who may quote and cite passages.

Key Words: learning styles, reflective learning, personality, introversion, extroversion, active learning, direct instruction, learning preferences.

FOR LANDON

CONTENTS

Introduction 1

Chapter 1: The Concerns 7

Chapter 2: The Constructivist Cause 15

Chapter 3: Personality Theory 23

Chapter 4: Learning Styles Theory 35

Chapter 5: Intercultural Differences 43

Chapter 6: Methods of Discrimination 51

Chapter 7: Instructivist Alternatives 63

Chapter 8: Original Findings 73

Chapter 9: Conclusions 91

Chapter 10: Recommendations 105

Epilogue: Story Tellers 113

References 119

INTRODUCTION

This book is for every reflective, introverted student who has ever had a course, or in some cases, an entire year of schooling, railroaded by a teacher who demanded they change their personality. Students are now exposed to what we call active or collaborative learning at every level from elementary school to the university. In the last twenty-five years there has been a growing awareness of this type of learning, sometimes known as constructivist pedagogy. The term constructivism is an umbrella for many terms and takes many forms, but its overall mission is dedicated to the idea that learning is an active process beyond thinking, reading, and writing. Social constructivist theory focuses on student interaction within the social context of an activity such as a small group or whole class discussion. Many education scholars believe students learn better in collaboration or through socially active discussion.

There is no doubt we have improved our classrooms with more interactive, collaborative, and learning-centered approaches. After all, we know the importance of engaging the student is critical to their success as a learner. For the English classroom, the social interactive process is generally standard practice with peer review workshops, group projects, and student presentations. As an English instructor at multiple levels from middle school to university, much of what I have done through the years with my students involves social interaction. Therefore, this book is not a directive for every teacher to stand at the front of a room talking from their notes or from a PowerPoint for seventy-five minutes.

One socially active learning method is the Socratic Seminar where students sit in a circle and discuss a topic or a text. A seminar always yields some students who excel in lively discussion, but there are always many more who remain quiet. There is a gross assumption that quiet students are not thinking about the work, that they are somehow unprepared, or have neglected their studies. However, students who do not vocalize their thoughts have their reasons. One significant and natural reason these students remain quiet is because they may have different personality types and learning styles. With a growing recognition of learning and personality theory, it is questionable whether every student truly benefits from teaching methods that demand real-time responses from students in a social learning environment.

One aspect of the social classroom is the idea of cognitive dissonance. Some writers have argued that learning takes place through cognitive dissonance resulting from mental disequilibrium. This means the student is thrown off balance and their peaceful state is infringed upon in order to "teach." This disequilibrium is one result of social discourse in the classroom. Those who support this aggressive approach claim that mental disequilibrium leads to a heightened state of understanding. Some supporters have also admitted they feel a need to make learning uncomfortable at times. However, other possible results include students who become alienated, become lost in the course, or even drop out. Cognitive dissonance does not recognize learning and personality differences, and the notion that we must be forced into a zone of discomfort in order to learn is concerning.

Collaboration is necessary in the real world. Entire governments would collapse. Corporations would cease. World peace would turn to chaos. The benefits of collaboration in a learning environment cannot be denied. Collaboration has value, but it's not the only way to accomplish things. We should not forget that many great accomplishments and creations have come from individuals.

Something often heard in teacher evaluations is how much students do not like group projects and how much they struggle with relying on others in the classroom setting. Imagine a student landing in a class that does all that and only that: group projects and collaboration? Yet schools of education are actually promoting this nightmare scenario. It would be unfortunate if an instructor used only one methodology without differentiating instruction for the other groups.

My research on this topic began in 2008. Originally, I wondered about teaching methods based on a hunch that I could not articulate or even identify. As I reviewed the literature in the psychology field and contrasted it with the literature in the education field, something clicked in me and I was suddenly aware that what I felt as a graduate student and what some of my students expressed to me along the way were all very normal reactions to the teaching methods we are subjected to. I began to read more. I embarked on teacher and class observations. I spent months in the local high schools, and I interviewed and surveyed the teachers. I then interviewed colleagues and instructors at the colleges I worked at. My official research study gauged the experience of urban college students subjected to different teaching methods, which I detailed in my last book *Learning and Personality*.

This new book *Personality and Prejudice* adds to the body of research concerning learning preferences in the role of teaching and learning, and to a small body of literature on reflective learners. I would like to believe this book is more accessible to the common reader than my last. This book is also a call for action. This book aims to show how students with more introverted personalities are affected by different teaching methods, one socially active and the other teacher-led. In lieu of surveying a large sample of the population, my goal was to document the student more in-depth and get closer to the student experience than a larger quantitative survey could. This was an opportunity to hear student's thoughts directly, instead of through the filter of a theorist or philosopher.

What I found was a collection of problems in education that left me with a mass of data on the cutting table, too broad, too complex, and too controversial to include even in a doctoral dissertation, my previous book, and this present one. With over four years worth of interviews, surveys, and observations of students and instructors from seventh grade to community college, I had collected a massive amount of data. What follows is only a portion of the data, which documents the experience and struggle of the introverted reflective learner in a world that values and rewards extreme extroversion.

Some theorists oppose a knowledge-based education and transmission of information by a teacher. They see education more as a development of skills. Because both the lecture and direct instruction have a component of knowledge acquisition, both methods are confused and demonized. Of course, direct instruction is not the same as a college lecture. Though the student-centered-skills debate brings a polemical fire, we should resist the oversimplification of such a complex learning environment with so many variables. Some students are more introverted and intrapersonal whereas others are more extroverted and interpersonal. Some prefer to learn via observation and reflection whereas others prefer to learn actively using experimentation. These factors seem to expose the lingering question of how one learner feels and thinks in a class designed for another. The emphasis on interpersonal active learning has now led to neglect for intrapersonal, introverted students who learn better independently or through direct one on one instruction. My research makes me concerned that we have arrived at a point in history where theorists have settled for one way to appease the restless 21st century students—through hype and sensation. Hence, we have a talk show type of education. Step up on the stage, talk loudly, and pretend you're getting an education.

1. THE CONCERNS

A growing constructivist movement that suggests a high level of student interaction fails to ever consider whether there are some students who do not benefit from more socially active learning. There is a legitimate concern for interpersonal skills and learning-centered education, but this concern has unfortunately led to neglect for intrapersonal, introverted students who learn better independently or via direct instruction. Some learning style theorists believe students may withdraw or become alienated in a class or discipline that demands the opposite learning style. [1]

In the context of my own English classes, there are various ways we approach the teaching of writing. No one would advocate one method of teaching all of the time, but we must wonder how many methods or approaches do teachers adopt without thinking about how the student feels. English teachers naturally use many methods that support the constructivist philosophy, but to what degree are these forms of engagement beneficial to all students, and what about the students who shut down under these conditions?

As an English instructor who has taught at different levels from middle school to the university, I have observed students who struggle when I put too much weight on discussion, collaborative projects, and student-led seminars. I have had many students, including some with physical disabilities, who did not want the entire class staring at them. Many expressed how "turned off" they were by an interactive, cooperative learning environment. Some of these distraught students in my more "student-centered" composition part II courses had previously excelled in my previous part I composition course, which is more "teacher-centered."

I have seen introverted, reflective learners shut down in the more "student-centered" settings. Along the way, some students sadly disappeared and withdrew from the course. One student with a disability even described his anguish to me in private, and I allowed him to write an essay about the experience instead of making him do the next oral presentation assigned on the syllabus. I have since modified my courses to have more of a balance of approaches, but I still wonder about these types of learners in other faculty members' courses who utilize all or mostly social constructivist methods.

Through the years, my colleagues and I have been bewildered over quiet students: why are our students so quiet? Is there something wrong? Are they unprepared? Are they apathetic? Are they just expecting to be spoon-fed their education? Of course, we cannot force students to talk, especially if we expect genuine interchange. Every teacher wants students to show some sign of life and reaction, but if we simply dismiss these quiet students as indifferent, lazy, anti-social or any other negative definition, we may be missing the real issue.

Some of those quiet students may be disengaged, some may be unprepared for class, but a good number of them are likely just introverted personalities who prefer to reflect and observe, or think and speak later. Introverts need time to form and articulate opinions, and there are valid biological reasons for this.[2] Therefore, punishing introverted reflective students and labeling them "passive" is a form of gross discrimination.

Since we vary in our preferred learning style, teaching methods should value variety and diversity.[3] Teachers should be flexible and take into consideration the different learning styles as well as personality types.[4]

However, teacher-led instruction is not the favored approach by scholars and has been "the particular target of disdain among educators," according to researcher Jennifer Goeke.[5] Even though students may be thinking, observing, writing, and questioning during teacher-led instruction, this type of learning is considered passive within the constructivist pedagogical framework.[6]

Education theorists believe teacher-led instruction is boring and rote. Less documented and experimental strategies are actually more popular in schools of education, and thus the many schools they influence.

The importance of self-reflection is well established, but students are not provided enough time to do so in learning environments that are too fast paced and socially active. Two studies determined that students who are self-regulated or have good forethought, performance control, and self-reflection performed significantly better in their course work than those who had little self-regulation and only possessed partial forethought and self-reflection.[7] Certainly it is hoped we are not punishing those reflective students who perform better just so we may accommodate others. Perhaps we ought to be improving those who struggle rather than changing the expectations for everyone.

Seventy-nine percent of the student population in one study[8] was found to be the type of learner who does not benefit from active learning. Judging by those numbers it would seem we are catering to just over one fifth of the population and leaving out the majority. It would seem our ambition to accommodate the extrovert or kinesthetic learner has swung too far in the other direction. Teachers are now neglecting a large number of learners in an effort to meet the education field's expectations of "active" learning because they assume everyone is like those few.

In her 2012 book *Quiet,* Susan Cain argued that American educators have been on a streak of favoring interpersonal extroverts.[9] Diane Senechal also contended in her 2012 book *Republic of Noise* that there is bias in favor of social activity.[10] This societal emphasis on interpersonal relations is rather recent in history.[11] Part of this reason may be because introversion is so grossly misunderstood with harmful stereotypes and societal prejudice.[12] There is a widespread assumption that introverts and thinkers are peculiar and abnormal. In opposition to these assumptions, Anthony Storr argued in his 1988 book *Solitude* that "learning, thinking, innovation and maintaining contact with one's own inner world are all facilitated by solitude." Pat Galagan pointed out in a 2012 article how despite a large number of introverted creative people, schools and workplaces do not provide an opportunity for those to reflect in their own private space.[13] Is anyone in education listening to these critics?

The literature on learning styles suggests that forcing all students to participate verbally in class has the potential to deter a good portion of otherwise capable and intelligent students. Yet haven't we heard experts in the field of education speak as if active learning methods are the only way students learn and that any other approach is outdated or wrong? These dismissals of other learning approaches may be due to a misunderstanding of personality type. For example, although introverted learners may appear uninvolved, they may be actively listening and reflecting.[14] To believe a learner is uninterested because they do not talk is quite a gross assumption.

While much attention has been devoted to accommodating extroverted students in recent years, little attention has been devoted to students who are more introverted because there is an assumption that all students learn through interpersonal activity. However, one study actually found the most common learning style was comprised of "Assimilators," those students who learn best by reflecting and watching.[15]

Group learning can be an excellent form of instruction when paired with whole class teaching methods, but it can be disastrous when applied alone. Susan Cain acknowledged how cooperative learning can be effective when in moderation, but also concluded how great teams are a healthy mix of introverts and extroverts. The problem is the education field does not acknowledge this healthy mix. Everything is about collaboration. Cain explained that a "shift from I to we" is being practiced in our schools with cooperative and small group learning where rows of individual seating have been replaced with pods of four or more desks pushed together. As Senechal pointed out, school administrators now expect instructors to incorporate group work into their classes. While collaboration is certainly important, not enough attention is being put on knowledge, independent thought, and attentive listening. Senechal explained how many high school administrators are actually requiring group activities because these provide an opportunity for all students to talk and talking is what is valued.[10] However, this enforcement of group work in schools can be physically and mentally painful for introverts.

Despite popular opinion, research shows that introverts do their best talking in anticipation and not on the spot.[16] Expert Barrie T. Pennington argued that group work is a system that excludes ideas and "is driven by personality and ego."[17] Small group work does provide more opportunity for student discussion, but there is a danger that more extroverted students will dominate these activities.[18] Some theorists claim that grouping students methodically is the key, but again this is a theoretical assumption that neglects to consider the true nature of extroverts and introverts. Author Sophia Dembling went as far as to argue that it would be difficult to find an introvert who can think clearly in the noise and chaos of a brainstorming session.[19]

Despite the psychology research, the majority of education schools in America promote more extroverted and collective activities, and the education journals are on the bandwagon. An open subject search in the *Education Research Complete* database will generate over 4,000 hits for "collaborative learning," over 4,500 hits for "cooperative learning," and over 7,000 hits for "active learning." There is a great deal of attention being put on constructivist approaches by the scholarly community and very little on the alternatives, regardless of the concrete results in other social sciences.

Part of the rationale for social constructivism is to build community, which is also undoubtedly important. However, as Lawrence Cremin noted "community is more than a collection of groups" and that some level of individualism is actually required to attain community.[20] Some of my concerns about group work in schools lead to the debate over individualism and collectivism.

Looking back in time, historian Thomas Davidson recounted how savages and barbarians were collective groups.[21] Free individuals had no place among savages. The savages were smaller groups that eventually gave way to larger groups consisting of barbarians. We historically evolved since barbarism, and as Davidson argued, "As men ascend above barbarism, their progress is marked by a gradual emancipation from institutions or a gradual development of individualism."

Individual ideals emerged: the hero, the saint, and the individual citizen in Greece brought forth the foundations of democracy and freedom. The British Romantics brought the value of individualism back from the dead. The American Romantics revived the spirit with Emerson's "Self Reliance" and the Beats in the 50s followed. Where is individualism now? Why has it been under attack for decades? And who seeks to regress us back into barbarians and savages?

2. THE CONSTRUCTIVIST CAUSE

Constructivist philosophy has dominated education for nearly a century with many of the same recommended strategies ebbing in and out under a new name every decade or so. The theory has two separate branches. One is how people construct knowledge through individual construction, everything my writing student must do as they research and write a paper. The other is how they co-construct knowledge with others, which is known as social constructivism. It is the latter version that is examined in this book and is best seen in the classroom seminars that elicit discourse.

Within this movement of constructivism, an argument seems to have developed into a false dichotomy of active learning or no learning as defined with various buzzwords. Constructivist pedagogy has been defined as teaching that "emphasizes the active learner— who discusses, questions, debates, hypothesizes, investigates, and argues in order to understand new information."[22] Anything other than constructivist is defined as "passive, rote, and sterile."[23] Education scholar E.D. Hirsch explained that educators from a naturalistic philosophy are caught up in a rehash of the "activity movement" that argues "all real learning is constructed" and direct teaching is unnecessary and unproductive.[24] Any approach that is concentrated with subject matter is demonized, while valuable time in schools is wasted on empty activities to fill time and appease students.

Education author Ken Robinson's animated YouTube video "Changing Education Paradigms" is celebrated in some schools of education for his criticism of a "factory model" of education, a disdain for facts, and his exclamation that "great learning happens in groups."[25] Robinson insisted that when we separate students and judge them independently we form a "disjunction between them and their natural learning environment." However, reflective learners see the instructor as the expert and often avoid interaction with peers.[26] It is also very much possible to still have a factory model of schooling that happens in groups with an interpersonal emphasis within the loud social constructivist paradigm.

Edgar Dale is an oft-quoted source of justification for socially active learning and has been immortalized by the school of education community. Dale created what he called a cone of experience to show a continuum of experiencing audio-visual media. Dale was attempting to provide a theoretical model and did not base his theory on any primary research.[27] Although Dale never attached any numbers or percentages to his cone of experience, others have mistakenly done so and renamed it the "cone of learning," a term that garners up over 14,000 hits on a web search and has been repeated in hundreds of scholarly articles.[28] Conduct a simple Google search and you will find dozens of images of cones or pyramids with Dale's cone of experience and the fictitious percentages attached to them.

The attached percentages first appeared in 1967 in a non-scholarly, film-audio-visual magazine article. The article was not written by a person in education or any kind of scholar for that matter. The author simply worked for an oil company and wrote articles on the side. Little else is known about this person named D.G. Treichler. What we do know is many prominent education and psychological theorists took the numbers and ran with them without actually checking the sources and credibility. It has since been perpetually repeated that we remember 10% of what we read, 20% of what we hear, 30% of what we see, 50% of what we hear and see, 70% of what we say, and 90% for what we do. However, this statement is actually not tied to any original data or sources.[29] No original study actually exists.

The percentage claim is grossly misleading as well as invalid because it has never been proven with any scientific study, yet it is widely accepted as truth by many in the education community. I can't tell you how many professional development presentations I've personally attended where a very credible and respected scholar or school leader used this falsification as evidence for their arguments, most likely unknowingly. To perpetuate such a myth, while we preach about research, credibility, and logic to our students is hypocrisy.

As a result of these bogus percentages, educators have been able to push what they call "active learning" to the forefront with more student-led presentations and seminars. "Active learning" jargon now consumes the education environment. With these beliefs, the 70% of what we say is emphasized far more than the importance of listening and reading. By this theory, it would be assumed that listening and reading is passive and not active, but in defense of reading, English scholar Robert Pattison observed, "it seems clear that reading has no necessary characteristics of passivity."[30] In other words, reading requires heavy brain power. Others have agreed that readers are very active information processors and not just passive decoders and recipients of knowledge.[31] "Listening, reading, and pondering" are actually the learning preferences of introverted learners, according to expert Carolyn Zeisset.[32] If teachers teach according to the fictitious cone of learning, they are denying those introverted reflective learners their preference for optimal learning. If leaders and scholars continue to use these debunked claims as evidence for their theoretical arguments, they will perpetuate one of the biggest and most harmful lies in education.

This misinterpretation, or manipulation, of Dale's cone of experience has led to teaching approaches that value students who talk. Students who listen and read are surprisingly devalued in these teaching approaches, which seems antithetical to education. E.D. Hirsch argued that "in the information age, the key to economic and political achievement is the ability to gain new knowledge rapidly through reading and listening."[33] Both Hirsch and education critic Jonathan Kozol have argued that the state of literacy is a tragic threat to democracy.[34] The state of literacy is only made worse in schools by rushing through texts, which literacy expert Kelly Gallagher has defined as "readicide."[35] Gallagher fervently argued that schools essentially kill students' love for reading. This may be reflective in the number of declining readers every year.[36] Some theorists have argued for more auditory and visual assignments in composition classes such as newscasts and videos. While this approach has value and may benefit particular learning preferences, others have argued we are far off the track of effectively teaching reading and writing skills because of our philosophical influences.[37]

Furthermore, E.D. Hirsch has argued that the naturalistic, interpersonal, activity-based approach to learning, taken up by schools of education and organizations, has removed direct instruction of grammar, which has thus led to frustrated high school teachers who spend too much time teaching middle school skills and ultimately leads to college students who are unprepared for college-level writing. In his book *On Literacy*, Robert Pattison argued, "the norms of correct usage may be false, pretentious, and outdated, but they are the standards of literate behavior demanded in government, business, and the professions." Students simply cannot get ahead without the tools of Standard English.[38]

Hirsch conjectured the façade of "learning by doing" to be "among the least effective pedagogies available to the teacher."[6] Yet we also know that simply providing information is not instruction.[39] Whether we remember 90% of what we do is irrelevant to the problems in education, because all learning should lead to an active experience of producing something, whether it be a research paper or a rain barrel. That final product is the ultimate assessment, but everything else on the cone of learning is how we get to that point. Even Mortimer Adler, who celebrated active learning and guided discovery learning, acknowledged, "The most important kind of doing, so far as learning is concerned, is intellectual or mental doing."[40] Adler also addressed the need to accommodate individual student needs, but then contradictorily proposed to eliminate all electives, which certainly hurts many learners. Despite this glaring flaw, Adler still recommended using a variety of methods to reach students. As Hirsch pointed out, "effective teachers have always taught through a diversity of approaches." To assume only one method is superior, as many administrators and theorists do, is detrimental.

Some educators have suggested that we need to change our methods of teaching because students can no longer sit still and pay attention. Perhaps the inability to sit still, listen, observe, and ponder has been diminished due to cultural or technological influences. Media theorist Douglas Rushkoff warned of a society that no longer considers the past or the future, one where everyone, kids and adults, are stuck in a distracted state of present tense.[41] Some adults can be shamelessly seen with their heads down in their devices during lectures, speeches, and even artistic performances. What is the point in being there? Surely, some of us can and should multi-task at times, but is this approach to learning effective? Using our devices might not mean we are absent, but studies show otherwise. A Microsoft study found employees took an "average of 15 minutes to return their attention back to the previous task when distracted by email, instant message, etc."[42] Why would this be any different for the learner in a college course? Or a class at any level?

The point in mentioning this cultural shift is because new approaches offered by theorists often include some form of technology in the hands of the student. From clickers to I-Pads, these devices do hold some exciting possibilities. However, technology also adds to the attention deficit. For this reason, my courses are mostly "unplugged" and I actually discourage such devices. It is my personal belief that a student should be able to unplug for 90 minutes so they can better visualize, listen, speak, and have real-time real-world relations without the distraction of a device they give so much attention to the rest of their waking hours. It is also a matter of respect to the teacher and other students. Many teachers will agree with this simple philosophy of an unplugged classroom. Yet so many theorists hail technology as the best learning solutions. Instead of working to help those who become distracted, theorists have decided it is more important to help everyone become more distracted.

Regardless of technology, many theorists claim that there is active learning or no learning, but there are problems with this false dichotomy. Many veteran teachers have warned of using only active, student-centered learning.[43] Professor of Education Psychology John Sweller argued how Constructivist teaching techniques, where students must seek out information for themselves instead of being explicitly taught by a teacher, have been the favored instructional techniques among researchers for several decades.[44] The problem, Dr. Sweller explained, is that these "minimally guided instructional techniques were developed prior to our current understanding of human cognition." In other words, we now know better based on brain research. So what if these active learning methods labeled progressive actually inhibited progress? Researchers have recently found that active learning methods do not lead to more student learning in college-level classes.[45] Others have identified specific problems with collaborative, cooperative, and inquiry-based learning models[46] to be explored later in this book.

3. PERSONALITY THEORY

In the 1920s, world famous psychologist Carl Jung proposed a philosophy that defines people by two different modes: introversion or extraversion.[47] Jung further divided the two types into eight typological groups: (a) introverted sensors, (b) introverted intuitors, (c) introverted thinkers, (d) introverted feelers, (e) extraverted sensors, (f) extraverted intuitors, (g) extraverted thinkers, and (h) extraverted feelers. Because that is enough to make anyone's head spin, this book will focus only on the general terms of introversion and extroversion.

Jung explained the stark contrast between the two personalities: "The two types are so essentially different, presenting so striking a contrast, that their existence, even to the uninitiated in psychological matters becomes an obvious fact, when once attention has been drawn to it."[47] Extroverts were defined by Jung as those who become energized by others. They tend to be assertive, talkative, and feel bored when they are alone. Introverts were defined by Jung as those who excel alone with their imagination and prefer reflection to activity. Research identifies 1/3 to 1/2 of the population as introverts.[9] Sadly, we are neglecting this large segment of the population with excessive group work and external activities.

The popular literature and media exploded with articles about introversion in 2012 after Susan Cain's best selling book *Quiet* brought attention to the extreme extrovert ideal. Cain argued how we have lost sight of who we are due to a national ideal for extroversion in America. Dr. Laurie Helgoe also theorized that America is extroverted, and as result introverts are forced into adapting, going underground, or going crazy.[16] Today it seems that the more talkative people are rated as smarter, and even just the word "introvert" has been stigmatized.

In defense of introverts, Cain pointed to the fact that many of the people who change our world for the better are "quiet and cerebral." Most scientists, engineers, accountants, doctors, writers and artists have been identified as introverted.[16] Identified introverts include Abraham Lincoln, Eleanor Roosevelt, Warren Buffet, Gandhi, Rosa Parks, Bill Gates, Barbara Streisand, T.S. Eliot, Al Gore, and many other successful writers, leaders, artists, and thinkers. Cain pondered why we would not want more people like this? Moreover, why would anyone want to stifle individuals like this, and what status quo are they defending?

One can simply look to modern American healthcare approaches to see the value of the external over internal. Physicians and therapists are not paid to investigate inside. Your only option as a patient is to wait until your external physical symptoms warrant an investigation (sometimes too late) or seek out an alternative holistic or Eastern doctor who values the internal and the whole body, inside and out. Just like the respected internal, the concept and act of introversion is far more respected now in Eastern cultures where people actually live in collectivist societies.

With the portrayal of "bad boy" introverts in the 1950s like James Dean's character Jim Stark in *Rebel Without a Cause,* along with the trauma of the 1960s (a worthy collection of reasons to come together as people), Americans have been programmed to reject being alone. Now the technological age has put any fear of even being *seen* alone all to rest, since no one ever has to be alone again as long as they have a cell phone. Perhaps we are becoming more collectivist and the East is becoming more individualistic, and none of us are even aware.

Contemporary society is designed to accommodate and reward only the extrovert, and this starts in our schools. Introverted children have actually been identified as troubled and weak students. All of the things introverts prefer like lectures, independent projects, and time to reflect are being minimized in today's schools.

One research study described an introverted reflective learner named Judy.[48] The four year old would not engage in playtime with others, but the researcher later found that Judy was a very astute observer of the social politics. The child actually excelled in assessments that measured organizational skills, accuracy, and perceptiveness, but these strengths may have never been identified if she had not been a student in Howard Gardner's Project Spectrum study. Judy might have had a difficult time in school since most teachers believe that the perfect student is an extrovert.

Award-winning teacher and critic John Taylor Gatto articulated the effects of the extroverted ideal by arguing that the most educated are conditioned to "dread being alone" and seek superficial relationships through technology.[49] There is no doubt the extrovert ideal is being conditioned in our children from a very early age.

Introverts are misunderstood and castigated in western society. People in western society actually have a fear of solitude, and because of urban myths, like the introvert being a psychopath or the lone gunman, introverts have been ostracized in western culture. Scholar Jerome Kagan argued how "American society is suspicious of the introverted isolate with one or two friends..."[50] Parents now worry about their children playing alone.[16] Some of this fear and confusion has been linked back to Sigmund Freud, who considered introversion a form of pathological neurosis.[19] Sociologist Peter Callero went as far as linking individualism to egoism and selfishness and even pointed to extreme individualism with examples like the Unabomber, Ted Kaczynski.[51] Of course, most people, even radical thinkers, do not kill others for satisfaction.

If we used Callero's obviously flawed line of thinking we might point to the mob mentality of mafias, gangs, and hate groups, and argue that all groups are dangerous. Those groups have done atrocious acts and have terrorized society, but our argument would be logically flawed if we assumed all collectiveness is evil. We certainly have far more reason to fear groups than an individual.

Despite a reputation for being troubled, "not all creative people are notably disturbed; not all solitary people are unhappy," according to Anthony Storr. Introversion does not equate to psychological problems, anti-social personality disorder, or social phobia[16] nor does it mean someone is deranged or criminal.[9] Introverts have been passed off as an archetype for violent methodical criminals such as school shooters, but they are often the prime victims of bullies. It has been documented that many school shooters were both introverted and bullied, and it is true that in "12 of 15 school shooting cases in the 1990s, the shooters had a history of being bullied."[52]

We know that victims of bullying are often very low on the extraversion scale and that personality, while not a sole cause, does play a role in who bullies and who gets bullied.[53] Bullies are certainly able to "sniff out loners and nerds."[17] Of course, logic tells us that not every introvert is bullied, not every introvert goes insane, and not every insane person is introverted.

The negative perception of introversion seems odd in a nation that has traditionally celebrated self-reliance and individualism.[54] Ralph Waldo Emerson founded these American principles in the early 19th century when he argued:

> These are the voices which we hear in solitude, but they grow faint and inaudible as we enter into the world. Society everywhere is in conspiracy against the manhood of every one of its members. Society is a joint-stock company, in which the members agree, for the better securing of his bread to each shareholder, to surrender the liberty and culture of the eater. The virtue in most request is conformity. Self-reliance is its aversion.[55]

But Emerson should not be confused for an anti-social hermit, nor should Henry David Thoreau who wrote of going into the woods to live in solitude, even though he still had plenty of visitors and was only a short walk away from town. Both writers were active in society, but they also understood introversion. Emerson's philosophies have been part of the American intellect, but more and more are sacrificing their solitude for the comfort of collectivism.

The origins of hyper extroversion, in a culture of personality where we value those who entertain us more than the ones who inform us with facts and knowledge, come right from our Ivy League colleges. Susan Cain explained how Harvard rejected sensitive intellectuals as early as the 1940s in favor of boys of the 'healthy extrovert kind." Much of the abandonment of the internal also finds its roots in the world of psychology with radical and cognitive behaviorism.[16]

Cain examined historical examples of how the extroversion ideal originated with the Greeks, Romans, and then later with our outspoken founding fathers, and argued that early Americans felt threatened by intellect pointing to the 1928 presidential campaign of John Quincy Adams (one of the few presidents identified as an introvert) versus the extroverted military leader Andrew Jackson.[9] A Jackson slogan read: 'John Quincy Adams who can write/ And Andrew Jackson who can fight'. Jackson devastated him in the election and would go on to become one of the most ruthless presidents.

The collective trend in education that pushes for more and more group learning is not only annoying for introverts, but it can also be physically painful.[56] It has been well established by researchers that introverts prefer to talk to one person at a time and are uncomfortable in groups.[57] Introverts are often more sensitive[58] and in fact 70% of highly sensitive people tend to be introverts.[59] Introverts may be more distracted by "sirens, glaring lights, strange and strong odors and clutter."[17] Of course, siren-like bells, glaring lights, strong odors, and clutter are common in American schools, so introverts are already at a disadvantage the moment they walk through the door.

There are legitimate biological differences between introverts and extroverts.[2] Researchers Debra Johnson and John Wiebe used PET scans of the brain to show brain differences between the two personalities, which revealed that introverts have increased blood flow in the frontal lobes and anterior thalamus, while extroverts have more activity in the posterior thalamus and posterior insula.[17] Other research shows how brain scans reveal how extroverts are faster in decision response and faster in translating thought to speech; and the faster rate of thinking may be why more athletes are extroverted.[19] Therefore, verbal participation with seminars and debates do not appeal to the nature of introverted learners in a classroom setting.

Introverts like to take their time, polish and practice their work. They think slower, have sensitive sensory processing, and are the least likely to be narcissistic.[19] Most introverts are highly empathetic, passionate about their values, and even take the lead on social activism.[17] Jung once wrote: "They [introverts] are living evidence that this rich and varied world with its overflowing and intoxicating life is not purely external, but also exists within."[59]

To contrast the two personality types in simple terms, introverts are more like cats, while extroverts are more like dogs. The cat greets you quietly and calmly, while the dog greets you loudly and wildly. Pennington pointed out a misconception about introverts where "like cats, they can be simplistically dismissed as unsociable and unfriendly."[17] Ask the one third of the population who shares their home with a cat though and they might say otherwise. There just happens to be more domestic cats in the U.S. than dogs[60] so cats can't be that bad. Cats are more independent and dogs require more direct attention, but it does not mean either one is wrong.

Introversion and extroversion complement each other, but they are quite different.[61] According to Myers-Briggs, the introvert is more subjective and reserved. Introverts seek understanding and meaning while extroverts seek sensory stimulation. Introverts seem to be far more reflective, while extroverts are more active. David Kolb pointed to several longitudinal studies that show how personality type is one of the most stable characteristics throughout life.[1] However, Jung believed that we may also change from situation to situation in order to adapt and that we often grow more introverted as we age.[47]

Jung believed that "individuation is a natural necessity."[47] The capacity to be alone is an important skill that enables people to learn, think, be innovative, change, and imagine. Author Anthony Storr explained how "human beings are directed by Nature toward the impersonal as well as the personal."[11] Storr suggested that solitude is therapeutic and includes practices like prayer and meditation, which have little to do with other people. However, contemporary western culture is an obstacle for the peace of solitude. Too many people today fear solitude because they believe it is competitive or too individualistic, but even Callero, a critic of individualism, recognized that "modest expressions of individualism can be beneficial and constructive" and that some "social isolation can facilitate self-reflection and a sense of inner peace."[51] To what degree individualism is defined by may be debated, but the complexities involved with individualism should open up more inquiry into the group vs. individual crux.

Privacy, autonomy, and solitude equal creativity. Artists, as well as some of the greatest thinkers like Descartes, Newton, Locke, and Nietzsche, actually spent a great deal of time alone.[11] Yet it is questionable whether we provide this reflective opportunity in our schools. Even creative writing is taught as a group project in secondary schools today, although we would have a difficult time finding a published creative writer who writes with a single other living being in the room, or even the same home. This new groupthink bandwagon has the potential to suppress both creativity and productivity at work and school.

Now even introverted teachers are being stripped of their privacy and autonomy with collective assignments and assessments. Now common learning teams are supposed to decide what you do in the classroom, and the results are often cold, uninspiring lessons being taught by script-reading monkeys for hire.

As Diane Senechal warned, we are only getting louder as a society and the outpouring of emotions on social media is a great example of how extroversion has spread.[10] Extroverts are more responsive to external rewards, and a capitalist society that looks outward for rewards makes the establishment of groupthink a far easier task.

The ironic part is that those extroverted skills promoted in schools do not even translate to success in the real world, even in the business sector. One university study found that the CEOs of 128 major companies who were considered charismatic had bigger salaries but not better performance.[9] In fact, Cain reported how introverted leaders in one business study outperformed extroverted leaders by more than 14%. Studies also show that extroverted open space plans lead to hostile, insecure, and distracted employees.[13] Many businesses (e.g. Reebok, Backbone Entertainment) are finally just reshaping their organizations to allow more privacy, autonomy, and solitude.[9] Pixar and Microsoft are another two companies that accommodate the individual employee while also encouraging interaction.[9] Yet, schools are going in the opposite direction.

Through a series of interviews, Susan Cain found that college students in many programs now have to act forcefully to survive in their environment and talk with confidence even if they are unsure. Professor David Williams echoed this assertion of collegiate confidence and argued "The only difference between Harvard students and community college students is that Harvard students think they are right even when they are wrong, and community college students think they are wrong even when they are right."[62] If we value talk and confidence over intrapersonal skills in the classroom, what then are the societal results when these students graduate to the workforce?

Steve Wozniak, co founder of Apple, is another successful person Cain pointed to who is a solitary introvert. Wozniak wrote about the nature of introversion in his memoir *iWoz*, comparing engineers to artists and advising kids to work alone: "You're going to be best able to design revolutionary products and features if you're working on your own. Not on a committee. Not on a team."[9]

It is not my intention to condemn collaboration and teamwork. Obviously, working together is very necessary in our complicated world, but there has to be a healthy balance. When we fail to acknowledge personality types and assume everyone works better in groups, we leave out the thinkers, inventors and artists who have helped shape our world.

4. LEARNING STYLES

Various theories have been developed to shed light on various dimensions to learning, such as Howard Gardner's multiple intelligences (1993), David Kolb's learning styles (1976), Anthony Gregorc's cognitive style differences (1982), and various versions of Jung's psychological types (1921). The theory of learning styles has multiple versions and diverse origins. The study of learning can be traced back to 1904 to Alfred Binet's intelligence tests that sparked interest in student differences. Around the same time in 1907, Maria Montessori began her Montessori method of education in order to enhance and accommodate student learning. It would not be until 1956 when Benjamin Bloom introduced his taxonomy that we saw an interest in multiple levels of learning. In 1962, Isabel Myers-Briggs and Katherine Briggs developed their Type Indicator based on Jung's theory of personality types. Myers and

Briggs were the first to show the significant differences among different types of learners based on personality, particularly introverted and extroverted.

David A. Kolb began writing about individual learning styles in 1971, and in 1976 he offered his first version of the Learning Style Inventory. Kolb's Learning Style Inventory contains four quadrants of learning zones within a cycle that features four distinct learning styles on the inside. Rita and Kenneth Dunn introduced their version of a learning style in 1978, which brought in environmental, emotional, sociological, physiological, and psychological factors among the differences between student preferences. Then in 1982, Anthony Gregorc introduced his own model, which applies two perceptual qualities of concrete and abstract and then two ordering abilities of random and sequential.

In 1987, Neil Fleming launched his own version called the VARK model, which simplifies learners into just four categories of learning preference: visual, auditory, reading/writing, and kinesthetic. Fleming originally had three sectors in what was known as the VAK, but later added the reading/writing quadrant to complete the model. The VARK model remains one of the most popular to determine student preferences. Bernie McCarthy created his own model in 1990 called the 4 MAT model, which also has four categories: Imaginative, Analytic, Common Sense, and Dynamic. Several of these models feature quadrants, which is a concept that dates back to ancient times and has been seen in Hippocrates' four body liquids, Blake's four Zoas, and the medicine wheel in Native American wisdom.[63]

The Kolb theory, which originated in 1976, is an important theoretical base for all learning style theory. The theory was developed as a learning cycle based on Kolb's earlier 1969 research based on experiential learning theory. Kolb began by studying Jung's research that dealt with how people perceive and process information. Researchers Jones, Reichard, and Mokhtari explained how "Kolb based his theory of experiential learning on peoples' different approaches to perceiving and processing information, information integration, and nondominant modes of expression."[64] Kolb then took learning style research and formulated a model of types based on the Jungian concept of development. The model presents an experiential learning process based on "adult learning and group dynamics."[65] Kolb was sure to explain how "individual learning styles are complex and not easily reducible into simple typologies."[1] Previous research has shown that "learning styles are influenced by personality type, educational specialization, career choice, and current job role and tasks."[66]

Kolb's Learning Styles Inventory classifies learning into a cycle of stages. The complete Kolb cycle of learning stages contains four learning process zones (or cycles) on the outside of a sphere and four learning styles on the inside. Individuals would process information on a scale between hands-on experimentation and reflective observation.[67] Those who are considered reflective learners learn best by reflective observation, reliance on an expert teacher, and often prefer to work alone. David Kolb and Alice Kolb have described these reflective learners as students who "prefer readings, lectures, exploring analytical models, and having time to think things through."[68] Yet, as mentioned, today's school of thought in teaching colleges is more focused on active "student-centered" and cooperative learning.[6]

The primary concern with active learning is with the students who learn through Abstract Conceptualization and Reflective Observation, classified by Kolb as Assimilators. Assimilation learning style is parallel to introversion.[69] These introverted students are the least accommodated with active and group learning strategies. Reflective learners, those who learn through reflection and not right on the spot under the pressure of an on-demand performance, learn by observation and reflection and "see the instructor as the expert" and also "tend to avoid interaction with others."[70] They prefer abstract concepts and thrive off of reflection and observation.[71] These kinds of learners are less focused on people and prefer logical and factual lessons. They read and listen actively and do not require active learning methods.[72] Introverted reflective students do not like team building exercises and brainstorming sessions.[19] They rely on an expert and learn from past experience.[71] They learn by watching and thinking.[67] They prefer lectures and processing time to analyze different aspects of the information they have received. The research and literature shows over-whelming evidence that reflective learners benefit from teacher-directed lessons.

Students classified as Accommodators on the Kolb scale rely heavily on other people and are defined as extroverted.[1] They strive in group work and hands on learning.[72] They learn though doing and feeling. These individuals enjoy working in teams in order to accomplish tasks. They prefer concrete examples and active experimentation, and discovery learning is a perfect match for these learners.[67] The problem is they are only a minority of the population.

Studies show how Assimilators are often the largest population and Accommodators are often the minority, which means we are adjusting our teaching to benefit only a select few as we actually harm the majority. One study found that active learners were the least common at just 14.7%, and 8.8% of the control group.[15] Yet, today's teaching trends cater to this small group at the expense of everyone else.

The learning style experts tell us that individuals learn differently and that multi-dimensional teaching models should be used. It is important to note that even learning style expert David Kolb has reiterated that there is no such thing as a fixed learning style and that learning happens in a cycle.[68] One study found that compatibility of student learning styles with the teaching style of their instructors resulted in retention of more information when the styles match.[73] For example, poor first-year science instruction can be tied to failure to recognize learning styles.⁷³ This failure results in the loss of over 200,000 science students each year who switch to other fields after their first college science courses.⁷⁴ One study implied that "active learning is not a quick or easy fix for the current deficiencies in undergraduate science education. Simply adding clickers or a discussion to a lecture is unlikely to lead to large learning gains."⁴⁵ In other studies, direct instruction has been found to be highly successful for increasing success in multiple subjects.⁷⁵ Reflective learners, visual learners, and intuitive learners all benefit from direct teaching, so the implications of this book are significant.

There is a strong parallel between reflective learning style and introversion. Sofia Dembling, in her 2012 book *The Introvert's Way*, noted that for introverts, "sitting and watching is a complete feast" for their senses. Academic research backs this up and shows how these students prefer to work more with things and symbols and less with people.⁷⁰ In considering personality types as discussed in the previous chapter, along with learning styles and preferences, is it possible schools are discriminating against a large portion of the population?

The apparent discrimination against introverts may very well contain an element of other forms of discrimination, including sexism. Past researchers of learning styles have considered gender. Multiple studies have found differences between gender for learning style preference.⁷⁶ One study found that more males were Assimilators (those who are more introverted) than any other learning style.[77] One study even showed that males were more likely to be Assimilators and females were more likely to be the opposite.[78] It would seem if we are catering to only active learners, we may be neglecting most males since they make up a large portion of reflective learners. Our social teaching approaches may be one factor why boys are dropping out of high school and college at alarming rates. So the list of prejudice continues to grow.

While there may be a gender bias at work, I do not happen to believe this is the cause or even a worthy focus. After all, how do we explain the millions of introverted female students who are alienated in classrooms across the nation? I have personally surveyed many female students who were lost in the chaos of an active learning classroom. We could generalize and argue that males have been challenged by a feminization of education that dates back to World War II, but we could also easily point to the male edge in math and science. These generalizations do not help us. If anything, I would suspect that gender bias is an inadvertent effect of personality prejudice.

Another unintentional effect of personality prejudice is our mistreatment of certain college majors. David Kolb found that many business majors fall into the more extroverted learning style category of those who prefer to talk.[1] In contrast, the vast majority of art students in one scholarly study were found to be a more introverted learning style.[79] Other research found that the most populated group of learners consisted of students with more reflective and introverted learning styles.[80] Once again, if we are catering to only the active learners, we may be neglecting the majority of students.

Study after study found that the majority of students in both the university and community college setting were of the Assimilator learning style, which is the most introverted and reflective of the styles. These studies show that fewer students are as truly extroverted as we assume. Under the influence of constructivism, schools are catering to a small sample of the population who are kinesthetic learners (many of these are athletes, kids with ADHD, and overly confident fast talkers), while we neglect the visual, auditory, and intrapersonal learners who actually enjoy learning from a teacher. Besides some exceptions, American classrooms are becoming too over-stimulating for introverted reflective learners.

Examining all of the studies, it appears if instructors only teach to the more extroverted, they would only be accommodating the business majors and the least number of overall students. Art majors would be particularly vulnerable, but the majority of majors would be neglected under the status quo. The research findings suggest different learning styles are being neglected as a result of deliberate teaching methods. If we are favoring interpersonal extroverts and kinesthetic hands-on learners with our teaching methods, where does this leave the other learners? Where does that leave most learners?

5. INTERCULTURAL DIFFERENCES

One related and major part of this personality prejudice involves culture. I realized this through my experiences teaching international students. It was apparent that international students struggled with one part of the American classroom more than anything else: oral participation. At first, I assumed it was the normal language barrier. Then I assumed it was a kind of intercultural anxiety they developed. Next I started to wonder why not all international students had the same struggle; in fact, some students of South American and European descent did not seem to have the same struggles Asian and African students had.

Of course, there is always an exception to the rule—the Asian or African fast-talking student who loves to verbally participate. But I have come to find that one reason for international student stress is simply a higher number of introverts due to cultural origin.

I have always been cautious of generalizing one type of student into a classification or division, but I could not help recognize the struggle of so many international students. Student after student, each one struggled with seminars and discussion. They shook their heads in disbelief or stared off in confusion every time extroverted Americans went on and on in class with their opinions and feelings.

My experiences led me to the research, which revealed all the same problems I had been observing. Suddenly, I was reading case after case of international students finding themselves in very uncomfortable scenarios in American classrooms. Then I discovered the same problem existed for those students in other countries with a visiting American teacher. There did not seem to be an adaptation on the teacher's part. Western pedagogy seemed to demand cultural change from these students in an imperialistic manner, which is surprising since many branches of "progressive" education originate from the social justice background of Freirean Marxism. This philosophy examines societal oppression and even becomes a voice for the oppressed, yet the effects of the teaching it advocates is oppressing so many. This troubling revelation puzzled me.

Then I found that entire international programs in the U.S. were dedicated to indoctrinating non-native students so they could learn the American way. These programs teach international students about western education and how to assimilate, all with no regard for the student's culture. The acculturation strategies are aimed to wipe out who they are and make them fine American talkers (and consumers), which is certainly not how I define social justice. This approach to education is oblivious to the cultural influences on personality and learning style and it is absurdly obnoxious to believe we can just change these students. This goes way past skills and language preparation— this is the imperialistic destruction of another culture.

I can't imagine the diverse group of international friends I met during my state university experience in Portland Oregon having to go through this. They all brought their cultures to our city and we all adapted to each other. What a shame that so many international students today have to be subjected to this attempted programming. Whether the attempts to change people's embedded natural personalities are successful is another story; I doubt they do, but the attempts cause harm.

A community within the United States that feels the brunt of social constructivism in the classroom is the Asian American population. Most Asian Americans are from a collective culture that is quieter. In other words, their heritage makes them naturally more introverted and reflective. This makes them a prime target for personality prejudice.

Asian Americans are culturally more reserved in their speech and behavior, yet their motivation and concentration skills also often surpass other Americans, which I, and many others, have observed first-hand as an instructor through the years. Many regions of the U.S. have significant Asian American populations, and they represent over 17 million Americans according to the U.S. Census Bureau, so there are greater implications for this issue. Regardless of the number, no person should be discriminated against, in or out of American school.

Many Asian American students in American schools (and Asian students with American teachers) from K-12 to college level have a feeling of discomfort and frustration and often complain about having to sit through gibberish. This is because in these more introverted cultures, and likewise in the minds of many American introverts, the teacher is expected to be an expert. For these students, group work is unnatural, and leadership from a teacher is the expected norm.

Several studies found that Asian American students are more introverted and must contend with an extroverted and confusing American approach to education when being educated in the United States. Students find that credibility decreases as material is discussed without expert guidance, themes are taken out of context and meaning is lost as it moves further and further away from the primary source of study.

Many researchers have reported the shocked responses of Asian American students when they first enter American classrooms, either at the secondary or college level.[9,82] Many are taken back by the amount of nonsense that goes on during class discussions. In

American schools, the one who talks the most, the one who talks the quickest, and the one who talks with confidence, wins the game of acceptance.

There are some key differences between western and eastern learning, and this may have implications for American students from different backgrounds.[81] The 1999 book *Asian-American Education: Prospects and Challenges* documents how Japanese, Korean, Chinese, Filipino, and Vietnamese educations hold great emphasis on relation of facts and memorization. The book explains how Japanese education is routinized, teacher-centered, and textbook orientated, which constructivist scholars are critical of. Chinese students learn by listening, observing, reading, and imitating.[82] All of these ways of learning would be considered "passive" by Western education theorists.

The Asian American or Asian student is more acquainted with working on their own in the school setting, even though most of Asian society is a more collective one. Filipino-Americans are not used to working in cooperative groups; they are taught to be polite and encouraged to remain quiet.[83] Vietnamese are accustomed to lecture style and do not participate.[84] Korean students do not prefer to speak in class and hesitate when expressing their opinion.[85] Chinese immigrants "might be confused by the spontaneous and outspoken behavior of their peers in American classrooms..." and may "experience ambivalence and confusion in the [American] classroom."[82] Their lack of participation can easily be mistaken as apathy or incompetence. Likewise, Filipino Americans may be observed as not being assertive in class, and teachers may associate passivity in students with a lack of ability[83]

One study found that Korean Americans have a negative preference for group learning and tend to be the most visual of any race.[85] C.C. Park advised that "teachers should try to minimize the use of small group activities for Korean-American students."[85] Another study found a lot of learning diversity among Japanese American students, but found that these students "may consider loud, excited classroom dialogue improper or even boisterous."[86] One ESL study found that "introverts of Chinese, Japanese, and Korean (Confucian-based) linguistic background scored slightly higher in reading than extroverted students with similar language origin."[87] So to discriminate against these students, educators would actually be out to destroy the best readers.

Another study reported the challenging results of American and other western teachers in China who used a Western style pedagogy of "student-centered, communicative learning..."[81] Many foreign teachers ended up disappointed and even bitter over their unsuccessful endeavors in China. 70% of students in the study complained that the teachers were improvising and had a lack of organization and linearity, "which resulted in a lack of a sense of achievement for the students." Foreign teachers with the western style also received numerous criticisms for treating their students like kindergarten kids with their active learning methods, talking "wild" and not correcting errors.[81] An interesting finding in this study showed how Chinese students believed the foreign teachers had bias in grading where mid level students with likable opinions received higher grades on their writing than the top students with good language and structure.

The parallels of this scenario in China to teachers in the U.S. who emphasize too much active social learning is concerning because the approach goes against the nature of introverted reflective learners, many who bring their cultures with them to America. Most U.S. cities have thriving Asian populations and the top five destinations are New York, California, Massachusetts, New Jersey, and Illinois, all among the most populated states.[82]

My observation of Asian American students revealed they were more introverted and reserved, and just as motivated as the native non-Asians, though a generalization such as this must be tested through future research. Regardless, we need to be cautious of culture and teaching methods. Do we really want to slow down our most motivated students by pushing them into discomfort? As educators, are we really satisfied by pushing any student into discomfort?

There is a culture clash between learning styles and teaching styles for students who travel or immigrate to new countries.[88] In some countries like Belgium, students do not answer the professor's questions even if they know the answer, whereas students in the United States answer the questions even if they do not know the answer. A more sociable environment in U.S. classrooms poses a problem for many of those students from other cultures. Despite their claim for inclusivity, many American educators are either ignorant of these cultural differences or just hostile toward them with a demand that they adapt to "our" way.

As T.Y. Nishida noted "Although our schools claim to accept diversity, we lack a concrete approach to understanding our children's differences."[86] Perhaps we need to better understand both collective histories and individual differences.

6. METHODS OF DISCRIMINATION

The methods used by educators to inadvertently discriminate against so many students are heavily promoted, unknowingly I assume. Schools of education, private companies, high paid consultants, and now even government officials influence school administrators, who then promote the use of or even mandate these methods down to instructors. According to the experts, the three C words are the trinity of instruction that will heal all of education's wounds and teach all students: constructivism, collaboration, and cooperative learning. As discussed in chapters one and two, constructivism is the root philosophy of the subscribed methods, but collaboration and cooperative learning are its offspring.

Collaborative learning was coined by British educator Edwin Mason in 1968, but these principles were articulated half a century earlier with the early progressive educators[89] and some of the techniques date back to the one room school house.[90] It has been argued that both constructivism and collaborative learning are more philosophy than actual teaching methods,[91] but some scholars have defined constructivist strategies as anything interactive and collaborative,[92] a definition still quite open to broad interpretation. The collaborative approach to learning is beneficial to extroverts and the learning style that favors active experimentation because they learn best by teaching others and prefer interaction.[93] Several studies have shown how "learning style preference of the student influences the effectiveness of collaborative learning."[26] The problem is not everyone learns the same way as the select few students who have the learning style or personality type that benefits from collaborative learning.

Cooperative learning originates from the work of Kurt Lewin in the United States in the early 20th century and can be defined as an arrangement in which students work in mixed ability groups in cooperation to reach a shared goal.[91] Group work is the simple mixing of students in groups and both cooperative learning and simple group work, if done carefully, can benefit students in the learning process.[91] However, cooperative learning may not result in cooperation or a shared goal.[91]

Students with interpersonal intelligence "love cooperative learning groups."[94] However, author of *Teaching at its Best,* Linda Nilson pointed out that cooperative learning is a supplementary technique and should not replace lecture, whole class discussion, experiential learning and other means. Nilson also addressed how discussion can get monotonous after a while, especially since it only appeals to auditory learners.[72] It has been widely reported that many students do not feel comfortable, others do not pull their weight in contributions, and others simply do not get along during group work.[95] It has also been found that groups of four or more students actually lead to a loss in learning.[96] Some studies show how performance gets worse as group size increases and how individuals actually produce more ideas alone than when they worked in groups, with the one exception being online brainstorming.[9]

The Socratic Seminar is one method to promote social learning. The use of questioning as a curricula framework is an ancient method that Socrates used. Socratic questioning is a process for examining the ideas, questions, and answers. Students must speak in this setting in order to gain participation points. Many scholars defend this approach and claim it is critical for achievement and intellectual development.[95] However, one study described a seminar on Emma Lazarus' poem "The New Colossus" that led to a hostile contemporary debate about immigration.[96] The teacher reflected on some of the problems with this conflict: "it seems my students only become more narrow-minded when presented with an opposing point of view."[97] While healthy debate is a democratic necessity in society, not everyone likes conflict, and no one should be subjected to it for a grade.

The seminar brings students into a dialogue about a text or issue. Often, instructors remove themselves from the environment and become an observer. The students are either leaders, who facilitate the discussion, or they are participants. The objective is for students to engage in dialogue to explore an issue deeper than usual.[98] To structure a course as a conversation helps engagement and comprehension, according to some[97] but an entire educational experience cannot be one conversation. As Jim Burke pointed out, the challenge is to integrate conversation with skills and knowledge.[97] The pro seminar writers, however, do not consider, nor mention, personality types, learning styles, or learning preferences.

It could be argued that one problem with the dialogue objective in a seminar is that it does not accommodate all learning styles and personality types. Many writers have claimed that seminars are for the purpose of speaking and listening and that these skills are not connected to personality,[98] but how do we ever remove one's personality from their actions, interactions with others, and everyday experience? Perhaps dismissing the importance of personality is a convenient way of assuming that introverts are content with pretending to be extroverted in a setting that demands it.

If the objective of a seminar is to get students engaged in dialogue about opinions, then the seminar may be a great instructional tool. While I personally see this objective as important in any school setting, it may not necessarily be a good objective for an English course aimed at improving literacy. In an age where testing is more and more important while literacy skills are threatened by media, games, and other distractions, class-room time has never been as important. What is it the teacher is trying to accomplish in the lesson with a seminar? That is the question that best needs to be addressed. Both teacher and student need to be aware of this objective.

English at the college level is naturally less reliant on testing than other courses and levels, so the objective is never to prepare students for an exam. However, high school classes are moving away from writing and moving towards more fill-in-the-bubble testing. It is not entirely clear how seminars or other social constructivist methods contribute to test preparation or any genuine learning of writing skills for that matter. A communications class could easily justify a seminar. In a college writing course where the class meets less than thirty sessions, or in some cases less than fifteen sessions, there is a lot less time to prepare students for writing papers. Therefore, the limited time must be utilized effectively.

If students are not able to adapt to teaching strategies or practices not in alignment with their preferred learning style, they may be at a disadvantage in such classrooms. Truly successful teachers use a variety of strategies,[64] but social constructivists do not seem to value the kind of direct instruction that benefits introverted learners.[44]

Other types of active methods include inquiry-based instruction or discovery learning where students are largely on their own working toward discovery of principles and ideas.[99] Many have argued that inquiry-based instruction engages students.[100] Although these methods are sometimes beneficial and not necessarily always group work, these methods have also been found to actually distract learners and do not result in long-term memory.[101] E.D. Hirsch deemed discovery-based instruction as the "least effective pedagogical method in the teacher's repertory."[6]

Hirsch explained in his 1996 book *The Schools We Need* that the picture of a "lecture format, passive listening, mindless drill, and rote learning" is a "mere caricature."[6] The rhetoric of "hands on" project-based discovery learning is usually used to "imply disdainfully that visual and verbal learning is artificial and unengaging" according to Hirsch.[6] These prejudices, Hirsch asserted, affect disadvantaged students the most.[6] Hirsch is not alone though; this assertion is backed by research findings by dozens and dozens of sources. One study found that low-income graduates performed better from direct instruction than students who did not have the same teaching.[102]

In a controversial 2006 paper, Kirchner, Sweller, and Clark reported multiple studies that have found problems with pure discovery learning.[102] The studies found inefficient results with discovery learning and showed how guided learning had better results. They found that the more guided the teaching the more success the students had. Hirsch has called for more guided and model-based learning and argued that students become more interested by good subject matter than by a student-centered classroom.[6]

Remarkably, learning styles and multiple intelligences are often justifications for methods of constructivism. "Let's appeal to all learners," they argue. The problem is their methods are alienating a large portion of the population. Every time you make schoolwork easier for the athletic student by incorporating kinesthetic activities, you are losing the intrapersonal reflective learners who might be very low in the kinesthetic area. "Well, differentiate instruction," the constructivists argue. And while instructors should be differentiating as much as possible, it is not always feasible to do so in one class meeting to the degree of accommodating all students all of the time. "Well, then, have them all talk" is not really the solution to a much deeper issue: the fact that students are being thrown together in a classroom with other differing types of learners and thinkers. This is the crux because this kind of diversity is beautiful in so many ways.

Howard Gardner's theory of Multiple Intelligences is an influential theory in constructivism, and in education overall, and for good reason. Gardner asserted that we all think very differently and thus we all learn very differently as a result. There are various online assessments where one can determine their dominant types of intelligence. Gardner's Multiple Intelligence (MI) theory is included in Table 1 to show how the personal-intelligences work in comparison to learning styles and personality types. At the bottom of the table are the recommended teaching methods.

Several scholars have noted the obvious similarities between introverted, reflective learners and intrapersonal thinkers.[103] Like introverts, intrapersonal thinkers are the most private.[104] Many researchers have noted how intrapersonal thinkers prefer individualized projects.[105] Researchers have acknowledged that more intrapersonal students prefer individual instruction, while more interpersonal learners do better with games and collaboration.[104] Gardner's book *5 Minds for the Future* has been considered an "appeal for a new appreciation of introversion" according to Dr. Barry Pennington.[17] Gardener has warned how there is little attention given to intrapersonal intelligence and how intrapersonal needs are neglected in education.[106]

In his definition of intrapersonal intelligence, theorist Peter Smagorinsky inanely defined it as someone who seeks outs and benefits from therapy and learns from their mistakes.[107] With such a narrow and negative definition it is no wonder why people flock to an admiration of interpersonal intelligence. Of course, we should consider that cult leaders and con artists have plenty of interpersonal intelligence, so there are also reasons to be cautious of promoting interpersonal intelligence.[108] We should all be careful to avoid hasty generalizations in our definitions.

It is worth noting that no student should ever be boxed into any neat category and that there are always exceptions to every generalization. Carl Jung warned that no person is 100% introvert or extrovert if they are to remain sane. Anthony Storr explained that neurosis follows if extraversion or introversion becomes extreme where in extroversion we lose ourselves in the crowd of conformity and in introversion we lose our touch with the real external world. No one is limited to just one world.[61] Others have pointed out that we sometimes change personality types during different periods of our life or in different environments we find ourselves in.[2] Even though collaborative learning tends to favor extroverts, all students have the potential to work in different modes under different settings, and it is my belief that they should sometimes be nudged in new directions, just not to the extreme of being tormented in a classroom.

Learning style and personality type theories argue that there are different types of people who react differently in one setting. This embrace of diversity is essentially a constructivist value and is modeled in the concept of differentiated instruction. The problem is constructivists turn around and do the very thing they are preaching against: teaching to one type of learner.

Unfortunately, learning style and multiple intelligence theory have been used against the introvert to promote more extroversion.

As Table 1 shows, personality is cleanly divided between introvert and extrovert. Both learning style theory and multiple intelligence theory accommodate the two personalities evenly. The more introverted students are more intrapersonal, which coincides with their preference for observation and a need for reflection. Based on the research, these intrapersonal introverts prefer direct instruction led by a teacher.

No truly progressive education philosophy should exclude any student, especially for naturalistic characteristics that define the individual as a learner and thinker. As this chapter has demonstrated, educators consistently use narrow theory to discriminate against introverted students. Some of these theories are as old as a hundred years before civil rights, women's rights, and environmental laws were established. The theories are used to defend beliefs and fraudulent myths like the "cone of learning" as discussed in chapter two. Teaching methods have been developed around the theories instead of learning objectives. This means administrators and policy advisors alter curriculum, and teachers alter units and lessons, all to accommodate the particular theory they currently have faith in.

Most effective teachers use a bit of everything, but many stick with what they believe or what they were taught. Any instructor using only one theory to guide their instruction is short-changing many of their students. There is a problem when any one philosophy drives everything a teacher or leader does because they fail to be objective and are blinded by their beliefs.

In composition theory we see so many trends come and go, usually all traced back to one or two composition gurus who have sold a lot of books. The latest trend replaces and dismisses the last until it too is lost by a newer more "progressive" idea. These new ideas are not any more progressive as the comp ideas of fifty years ago; they're just newer. There are some theories instructors do not even touch because they are just not practical in a general education core course, though they likely wouldn't admit this. Meshing theory with practice is mostly a problem for students with teachers who live by the words of a distant theorist or some new bandwagon campaign.

Bandwagon labels like *active-learning, cooperative or collaborative learning, discovery learning, and student-centered learning* have become mantras within the education community, and have gone unchallenged. These arguments for social learning are often circular and built out of assumptions. Yet these arguments are often the only ones heard in schools of education and from the graduates who go on to positions of influence.

Table 1
Comparison of Learners

Personality	Introvert	Introvert	Extrovert	Extrovert
Learning Style	Diverger	Assimilator	Converger	Accommodator
Type of Learner	Visual & reflective learner watching feeling	Reflective learner watching thinking	Kinesthetic & action learner doing thinking	Social & hands on action learner doing feeling
M.I. Intelligence	Intrapersonal/ Interpersonal	Intrapersonal	Intrapersonal	Interpersonal
Teaching methods that appeal to each style	Direct instruction, lecture, small group work	Direct instruction, lecture, readings	Labs, practicum, independent work	Cooperative & collaborative learning

Note: This matrix is based on previous comparisons conducted by Margerison and Lewis[110], Kolb[4], Chapman and Gregory[71], and Nilson[72].

7. THE INSTRUCTIVIST ALTERNATIVE

Instructivism is the act of learning via instruction. Direct instruction or explicit teaching has been observed as the best means of teaching basic skills.[75, 111] Direct instruction has been defined as being skills-oriented with the use of small-group and face-to-face explicit instruction.[112] Direct instruction has been found to be superior to discovery learning.[113] Some experts have suggested that every subject, even college English, should use some direct instruction.[91]

Behavioral learning theories and a well-versed, repeated criticism of knowledge-based education that asserts "students are not empty vessels" have dominated the education field.[6] Despite the "empty vessel" arguments, there is evidence that direct instruction can help students learn actively and that "student controlled learning can lead to systematic deficits in the student's knowledge."[91] Reflective learners and introverts also prefer a teacher-led classroom and prefer to think rather than talk.[93]

Direct instruction is not a lecture as many assume, though a lecture does happen to have its place in college instruction.[72] David Jonassen, the late professor of learning technologies and educational psychology at the University of Missouri, made an interesting counter to the constructivist argument for problem solving and argued that if learning is problem solving then why not let the student figure out what to do with a teacher's lecture?[114] Lectures are a problem to solve for some students since they have to connect the lecture to their course reading and research, and often those connections are not spelled out for them explicitly.[114] Jonassen suggested that the preparation, the lecture itself, and post lecture connections could essentially be considered a process of discovery.[114]

If delivered well by a lively professor and if studied well by an attentive student, the lecture can be very effective in the learning process. Critics of this approach would argue that the liveliness and attentiveness are unnecessary. They would call the lecture an old relic and insist that people do not learn with lectures, even though they presumably did in their own educations. Most of the top leading voices against the lecture did quite well with lectures in the prestigious universities they attended.

What is it they have against their professors and teachers? Do they really believe they learned nothing in the classroom during their educational pursuits? What inspires such a rebellion from a person's own past and experience? Surely, a couple of old theorists did not influence thousands of educators to throw their own educational experiences under the bus. If their disdain for their own education is genuine, then why should we take the word of someone who is admitting they have not been educated the right way?

Now even many job descriptions proclaim that *"Blank and Blank is a Student-Centered institution. The successful candidate will be expected to join faculty and staff with a commitment to active learning..."* We can debate what this all really means, but it does not sound very welcoming of other personality types and learning preferences. However, there are now a number of voices that have recently come out against those group-think philosophies.

The lecture lives on though, especially in most large universities with lecture halls that seat well over one hundred students across many academic disciplines. Many disciplines other than education use the lecture as a main method for reaching large audiences. To split up even a class of fifty students into two or three smaller sections would be costly to departments and unsustainable for many colleges. Of course, some introductory courses like first year writing, many math courses, and all developmental courses greatly benefit from smaller class size. Most high school classes benefit from smaller class size too. If administrators were really serious about engaging, truly preparing, and retaining students, then they would implement smaller class caps that allow the teacher to use a mentor model of education. But other than these exceptions, the lecture is needed, regardless of what education theorists believe.

However, direct instruction goes past the traditional lecture. In a broad sense, direct instruction is any direct teacher-led lesson. Though there are multiple models, the basis of most direct models is the introduction/review stage, the development stage, guided practice, closure, independent practice, and then evaluation.[115]

Direct instruction derives mainly from two lines of scholarship and curriculum development. The first line of development refers to Direct Instruction or (DI), which was created by Zig Engelmann in the 1960's and later refined with others in the 1980s. This model consists of an "explicit, carefully sequenced and scripted model of instruction" and is supported by a "landmark empirical research study" with follow up studies that have spanned more than thirty years now.[116] The initial study in 1967 was called *Project Follow Through* and was the largest educational experiment ever conducted, and evaluated nine major approaches to educating at-risk students.[116] Only students taught with the Direct Instruction approach consistently outperformed control students on basic, cognitive, and affective measures.[116]

The second line is usually referred to as lowercase direct instruction or (di) and was coined in 1976 by Barak Rosenshine after he found a causal relationship between a set of variables and student achievement. [116] There have been various other variations of the direct instruction model developed by other educators. There is also a more recent explicit instruction model called e.i. (explicit instruction), which puts more emphasis on how students process and structure in-coming information.[5]

The learning benefits of knowledge and skills based direct instruction has been acknowledged and recommended by education psychologists as an instructional method that builds metacognitive knowledge and skills.[91] Procedural knowledge must be practiced to develop the knowledge of the disciplines, and though many misuse practice as drill, practice is not drill.[96] Effective practice is a procedure facilitated by a guiding teacher.[96] Veteran writing educator and author Jim Burke recommended a three step process for most writing instruction that begins with teacher modeling, moves to a communal practice, and ends with independent creation.[97]

Direct instruction helps students perceive links among main ideas and will help them construct accurate understandings.[91] Ample evidence shows that direct instruction helps students learn actively. Various research studies have shown how direct instruction leads to more student achievement and how students learn more and learn faster.[111] Direct instruction lessons are successful specifically in the teaching of a fact-based course like American history.[117] One researched case study found that direct instruction is effective in improving reading comprehension skills and reviewed the literature on other key studies that backed direct instruction.[75]

Several reading studies have also shown positive effects. An article from the Oregon Research Institute discusses a study that evaluated the effect of Direct Instruction and found that it had a positive effect on reading skills for Hispanic students. [118] A 2002 study found that a model based on Direct Instruction had a positive impact on English language learners.[119] A 2003 review of programs for English language learners found Direct Instruction to be among the most effective programs.[120]

The National Institute of Direct Instruction has argued that solid research has shown positive results for over 25 years in reading achievement.[116] One extensive policy report identified 34 studies where direct instruction methods were compared with other methods.[121] The results showed 87 percent of the post treatment means favored the direct methods.[121] One key factor to note is many of these Direct Instruction studies are strictly at the elementary level. Another element to consider is the difference between DI and di, direct instruction. Yet another aspect to consider is how direct instruction sometimes includes small group activities during the practice phase or in a separate extension phase.[122] The many variations make the success of this approach difficult to identify in a simple manner, but the varied studies are out there as a counter-voice to the philosophies of theorists and those who follow their mantras.

Others have illuminated the successful English classroom as one that includes modeling, instructions, and guided practice.[123] The most effective teacher asks the students questions regardless of method.[124] Using different types of questions: factual and verifiable, inductive (why, how), and analytical (connections to other ideas, comparison, social context) is critical.[97] One community college professor uses a careful balance of three teaching styles: directing, discussing, and delegating.[125] In the first part of the semester he uses primarily teacher directed style. He moves to discussion toward the middle of the course, and then finishes with delegation. All three styles include an element of coaching. Professor Thornton explained, "If students have little or no experience, a directing style is appropriate."[125] Thornton's approach is both reasonable and inspiring.

Award winning elementary school teacher Rafe Esquith explained his direct approach to teaching reading: "I know which passages I'll read aloud and which will be read by the students... My reading lesson is like an orchestra, and as the conductor, I have the job to make the instruments sing."[126] Ironically, Esquith's whole class approach to reading might be mistaken by schools of education as a passive, teacher-centered, and old-fashioned teaching style. His approach is not likely to gain attention from schools of education, but he gets success with his students. Although Esquith taught on the elementary level, perhaps the most difficult and important of all levels, his approach to teaching struggling readers and writers still applies quite well to upper grade levels or even developmental college courses where students are behind in their skills. Esquith asserted that learning is not easy, should not be easy, and requires a fair amount of work ethic.[126] Those values remain the same regardless of level.

Of course, a challenging learning environment does not mean it has to be an uncomfortable environment that disturbs the student into learning the material. Educator Jim Burke argued school should sometimes disturb,[97] and his "Talk a Mile a Minute" classroom activity might actually disturb introverts and reflective observation learners. Researchers have warned that too much dissonance in a classroom without adequate emotional support could have negative effects and actually impede learning.[127] Educational psychologist Richard E. Mayer called the idea of dissonance a constructivist teaching fallacy that assumes "active instructional methods are required to produce active learning."[128] One study showed an unsuccessful use of cognitive dissonance that left students more baffled than anything else.[129]

Esquith believes setting a positive culture is what every teacher needs to establish.[126] Setting a comfortable climate for the students and using differentiated instruction are the keys to reaching all students.[71] Even the time of the day affects student learning,[130] so what is needed is a lot of sensitivity to psychological needs, not disturbance.

But even with his embrace of dissonance, Jim Burke also explained how modeling is an important step in writing instruction: "I do it (teacher models), we do it (create one together), they do it (independently)."[97] This is the classic direct instruction model consisting of modeling, guided practice, and independent practice. Professor Thornton justified the direct approach: "The directing style teaches students to listen, pay attention to detail, and follow directions."[125] This is the starting point for every successful teacher-led classroom.

Multiple studies in several states have revealed superior results favoring direct instruction in various subjects in both elementary and secondary education. Renowned education scholar Barack Rosenshine argued that there is empirical support for direct instruction.[115] Though critics might label direct instruction as teacher centered, Jeanne Chall's broad research in 2000 revealed how "teacher centered" teaching produced higher achievement than other approaches and was more effective for students who are at-risk, minority, or have learning disabilities.[111]

As the early chapters of this book presented, many writers, psychologists, and learning experts have testified that direct instruction, teacher-led lessons, and transmission of information are *not* negative and are actually essential to productive learning, especially for introverted reflective learners, and sometimes particularly those students most in need. As Diane Senechal suggested "traditional teaching cannot be reduced to a single method" and should include a combination of approaches.[10] There is no reason why we cannot have a balanced classroom with various methods and multiple pathways.

Some researchers have identified direct instruction as a method that allows ample time for reflection.[122] Earlier studies support direct instruction across the board.[123, 124] Several studies have now shown negative results for Constructivist strategies like discovery learning and inquiry-based learning.[102] It appears that the methods of Instructivism now have the science to support them.

8. ORIGINAL FINDINGS

My primary research provided some rather obvious confirmations, but also produced some odd, unexpected realizations. All participants reiterated the importance of teacher-led instruction regardless of their learning preferences, learning styles, or personality types. Therefore, the instructor who uses a lot of active learning strategies may appeal more to the students who prefer kinesthetic learning while putting the majority of their students – who are not kinesthetic learners – at risk. To my surprise, some introverted students claimed they liked the student-led social learning, even though they did not perform very well in that setting at all. Fifty percent of the population in my college study had auditory learning preferences, which is in line with research done elsewhere. Yet all we hear from education scholars is how many students need hands on work. It seems we are favoring one type of learner.

Across several studies, it has been established that about 30% of the overall population are auditory learners, 65% are visual learners, and 5% kinesthetic.[131] Auditory learners prefer to acquire information through lecture notes, and active learning approaches to teaching and learning could pose a problem for these auditory learners.[132] All of the students in my study who identified a preference for auditory learning selected teacher-led instruction as either their first or second preference for classroom activity, and most auditory learners chose teacher-led instruction as their first preference of learning.

There was conflict among the perception and behavior of the participants. One participant, an introvert with visual preference (Laurie) said that an uncomfortable learning environment would be "having to talk all the time," and shared how she gets nervous in class: "Speaking out loud. It's just something I've had a problem with." Laurie then contrasted the teacher-led instruction versus the seminars and said teacher-led instruction led to "a better sense of the questions" because in the seminars "I feel like the student questions are opinion based and have to do with the readings and sometimes the other students get off track and then I don't feel like I have anything to say." Laurie, who ranked teacher-led instruction as her most preferred class activity, barely said a word during the seminars. Laurie even admitted to skipping class on presentation day. Yet despite all of this, Laurie still ranked seminars as her second most preferable classroom activity!

Likewise, it was observed that an introvert with an auditory preference (Miriam) remained quiet in class. She expressed how she was more comfortable in the teacher-led environment where she could just take detailed notes. In the seminars, Miriam said she could not participate as much as she would have liked to due to her nerves. Despite this, Miriam ranked seminars as her second most preferable learning environment, just behind teacher-led instruction.

Another introvert with an auditory preference (Dorothy) also expressed her lack of interest in social learning and exclaimed, "I hate public speaking." She claimed to love the teacher-led instruction and enjoyed listening. Dorothy contributed minimal participation to the seminars, yet like Miriam and Laurie, she too ranked seminars as her second most preferable learning method.

Yet another introverted participant with auditory preference (Bella) did not like talking in class and did very little of it throughout the term. Bella described her anxiety and a speech impediment that led her, like Laurie, to skip out on presentation day. Bella also oddly placed seminars as her second most preferable classroom activity, right behind teacher-led.

An introvert with an auditory preference (Anthony) also shared his problems with verbal participation in the college classroom. He described an uncomfortable learning environment as "Somewhere where I would have to be expected everyday to share something with the class." As a result of these feelings, Anthony participated minimally in the seminars, yet he surprisingly chose seminars as his number one preference.

These introverts boggled my mind with their fondness of the seminars, a method seemingly out of line with their personality types. But even one socially active learner who tested as an extrovert with a kinesthetic preference (Emily) described her discomfort of having to talk in front of strangers. She excelled in a solo presentation, but rarely contributed to the seminars, yet she still ranked seminars as her second most preferable method. Student after student, so many behaved nervously and quietly in the seminar sessions and expressed discomfort or no interest in speaking to others in a social setting, yet they ranked seminars high on the list of classroom activity preference. In some cases they even stated they would opt for more seminars in class if given the opportunity.

What explains this odd contradiction?

I can offer two possible explanations. First, some of these students may find some element of safety in the seminar setting. Since they can choose to speak or not to speak, perhaps they feel relieved that the teacher will not formally call on them, regardless of the points they lose for not participating. Maybe they are relieved because they are in a circle with others in the same boat. Maybe they can hide behind the more assertive extroverts who are far more willing and likely to speak up.

The second possible explanation for why these students may have ranked the seminars so favorably yet failed to participate or express their views in class is that they simply enjoy listening.

For the auditory learners like Miriam, Dorothy, Anthony, and Bella, all expressed a preference to listen. For Laurie, a visual learner, and Emily a kinesthetic learner, listening was still mentioned as a favorable part of their learning experience. In fact, their VARK scores showed that they leaned towards being auditory learners, scoring fairly high on this preference scale. The conflict between perception and behavior was perhaps due to a lack of understanding the purpose of the seminars. In regard to the seminars, Laurie said she did not learn anything about writing. Despite her participation in earlier seminars, a warm up seminar before any of the graded seminars began, and an assignment sheet, she says she would have liked a better written guide. Despite modeling by the teacher and pre-seminar practice, Laurie was confused over the whole process and did not understand the purpose of the seminar. Unfortunately, she was not the only student to voice this lack of understanding and clarity.

In fact, every participant had a difficult time finding value in the seminar to the development of their writing skills. Some participants questioned the value of the assignment altogether and many participants did not take the activity seriously. They claimed that too much time was wasted and complained that some members of the class did not contribute. The more extroverted participants appreciated learning about others' opinions, but did not see the connection to learning about writing.

Counter to my expectations, and unlike the other introverts, Joseph participated quite actively in the seminars and teacher-led classes. He participated verbally in all of his classes and engaged in a great deal of thoughtful dialogue with his peers. As a reflective learner with a kinesthetic learning preference, he ranked teacher-led instruction as his third most preferable, only one of three to rank it so low. Yet despite his participation and high ranking of the seminar, he admitted the method was doomed without active student participation. He also expressed skepticism about how much they actually learned about writing through such interactions. The other two participants who were fairly verbal in the seminars, an extrovert with an auditory preference named Suzy and an introvert with kinesthetic preference named Richard, were socially active learners. Unlike Joseph, both praised the seminars as being extremely educative experiences. However, both had the same concerns Joseph had about low peer participation.

There are vast differences between how introverts and extroverts function and learn. Most of the introverts lived up to the definitions, or stereotypes of their personality type. But a few were far more assertive and sociable than expected. As mentioned, many of the introverts ranked the seminar high on their list of preferable methods.

As mentioned, the VARK, which measures learning preferences, was an added variable to my research. VARK examines how individuals take in new information as opposed to how they process the information. Half of my participants were revealed to have auditory preference, meaning they prefer to take in new information by hearing it. Only thirty percent of the participants had a preference for kinesthetic learning. Keeping in mind that this was a small study focused more on qualifying the experience of a few select students, no participants had a reading/writing preference.

The learning preference findings did not show any significant connections between personality and learning preference. However, auditory preference among more introverted reflective learners was the most significant and warrants further research. The auditory learning preference of the majority is at odds with the constructivist claim that we learn by saying and doing. The constructivist theory puts a lot of weight on kinesthetic learning by doing, yet my study, and many others, have only produced a minimal number of learners with kinesthetic preference.

Where the social constructivist theory is most challenged in these findings is in how the participants struggled with clarifying their learning objective, regardless of the enjoyable experience most had.

The success of the social learning model through a seminar was in how the participants enjoyed listening, though not necessarily contributing to the dialogue.

As noted earlier, solid English instruction contains constructivist approaches to learning in so many ways. Students build their written papers from the ground up, sometimes in collaboration, but often alone late at night racing to a deadline. The concern that evolved in this study was how the more reflective students reacted to social constructivist approaches. In the context of lessons that focused on learning about the elements of an essay, most students said they benefitted from the teacher-led instruction.

Most of the introverts were more reflective and reserved, as reflected in the literature. There was no direct comparison among the students regarding performance. Some participants seemed to thrive in some conditions, while others seemed to have floated through activities. The only conclusions drawn in this study relate to their personal experience and perception of differing methods. This study has confirmed a level of student dissatisfaction with social learning at the college level, particularly with introverted reflective learners. What the results might look like in a doctoral course, a high school class, or even a weekend community class might be different.

The participants' perception of the methods is clear, though it should be noted that perception could be deceiving.[133] Just because a student enjoyed one classroom method, does not mean they learned better, or learned anything for that matter. What if a student preferred the seminar because they felt they could escape direct questioning from a teacher? But what does that mean for their learning? The answers are limited. Even if the students were truthful in their responses and even if they were conscious of the limitations of their own responses, there is no way of connecting their narratives to performance.

This study did not determine actual performance, which could be studied in the future using a mixed methods approach. What this study accomplished was to elicit how they felt under certain conditions of learning, the different kinds of activities in the classroom. How those conditions change from day to day, from instructor to instructor, from course to course depends on multiple variables not possibly acquired in one course in one semester. The small sample warrants further research to determine if the trends observed in this study are legitimate across a broader more diverse American population.

As expected, there was a difference in how students perceived the learning environment associated with their identified personality type and learning style. The extroverts favored the solo presentation and seminar, while the introverts favored the teacher-led instruction and the seminars. The seminars were favorable to most despite confusion over the purpose of the activity. Solo and group presentations seemed either feared or disliked by most students. Revealing student frustration with these methods is an important step in addressing student needs in the English classroom. However, the importance does not lie in just pleasing students and making it easier or more comfortable; the importance lies in how much they're learning and what they are learning. If spending preparation and class time for presentations or seminars is going to be justifiable, then it needs to be connected to one of the major objectives of a writing course. While a presentation can be justified as a product of the written paper the student has just completed, a seminar is more involved in the pre-writing stage where the student analyzes writing models.

Seminars might be useful as a tool for that type of literary or rhetorical analysis when engaged in the study of professional essays, but the trouble is they require time and the discussions sometimes ramble off into non-academic directions. To succeed at seminars, the supporters tell us we need to do more and more of them, but that means less and less time where students are actually being taught by a teacher.

My research findings suggest that introverted, reflective learners respond differently to learning activities that are social. They may find social constructivist methods more difficult to learn from than non-social teacher-led presentations. In contrast, if a teacher does all the talking the extrovert may not have the opportunity to share their voice with the class and may not feel good in the classroom. These students might not be able to work through their thoughts without orally verbalizing them.

Perception versus behavior, and confusion over the objective are at the forefront of this study's findings. The elicitation of opinions in an English classroom appeals to democratic education theory where students are prompted to make connections between the content and their own personal lives. The seminars may have accomplished the task of getting others to discuss culture. However, this was not the objective of the seminars in this course.

The participants in this study seemed open to sharing with others, even if they were confused. On one occasion several participants even recalled the difficulty relating to a Latino author who wrote one of the assigned essays. Conversational learning could be seen as an experiential learning process where learners move through the four cycles.[134] It would be difficult to determine if the students in this study actually went through different cycles, since the students were not specifically examined for which learning phases they cycled through. Most of the participants lacked an understanding of the seminars—what they were supposed to be getting out of these classroom discussions, regardless of the instructions provided. Because different types of lessons ultimately require different methods,[135] I am unsure whether the seminar was a successful method to teach students about the features of an essay.

In contrast, the participants in my study valued the teacher-led modeling and had more confidence in this method in terms of reaching a clear objective. A teacher-led lesson might be used to teach the more specific form or structure of writing. Even democratic education theorist Susan Jean Mayer acknowledged how teacher-led learning "is most appropriate for demonstrating to students how to think about or to accomplish something in close to the same way as others have before them."[135] The teacher-led instruction offers a simple informative approach to the same lesson. However, teachers are told that "good" teachers "should 'negotiate,' 'facilitate,' 'co-construct,' 'mediate,' 'socialize,' 'provide experiences,' …but never ever will they tell."[136] I wanted to provide experiences, but too many of the participants had empty experiences.

Like collaborative and cooperative learning, there is more student-to-student reliance in the seminar and less teacher intrusion, especially if the teacher steps out of the seminar as I did. It is important to consider that fifty percent of the population ranked group presentations as the least preferable learning method and the other half ranked it as second to last. However, seminars were ranked in second place by the majority. This indicates a significant difference between the seminar and presentations. Such dismal rankings may indicate a justification for a decrease in application of this type of learning activity. If we suppose students ought to work through their frustrations and complete tasks that are less favorable, then perhaps group work is justified. How student preference should or should not drive instruction is debatable.

The words of the participants stand on their own as a testimony to how they perceived and coped with varying teaching methods in a general education college classroom. Because this study only involved a small sample of students, a future study could expand the size of participates and could be used across different instructors in different disciplines across various teaching communities. One element to keep in mind is that other instructors may change their instruction due to the Hawthorne effect if they know they are part of a study. Other instructors might also be better or worse at using direct instruction methods. Time, setting, and student variables are also considerations.

Constructivist treatment of the introvert and reflective learner did not conclude any better in my follow-up study at a high school. I thought the seminar would be more at home in English Language Arts classes that focused on literature instead of composition. The sampling was far greater this time, and the population was upper middle class in contrast to the urban college students I had previously studied. Racial diversity was also greater this time due to the location of the study. I was convinced these results would be completely different from the college study. I also assumed the high school students would enjoy seminars and excel at them better than the college students because they had more time to adapt to them during a whole year opposed to just a semester.

The results were surprising. An initial exploratory survey revealed that 27 out of 44 students disliked group projects. That's more than half the population of students that dislike group work in a school where the principals mandate group projects! 10 out of the 44 disliked class discussion. While that number is not quite as high as the first, it is still a significant number of students who may feel forced into discussion that rubs against their natural learning preferences.

The main portion of my high school study observed and surveyed 125 tenth and twelfth-grade students. Just over half of the students, 52.8 percent (66 students), ranked teacher-led lessons as being the most educational setting. In contrast, only 4 percent chose group work as the best environment for education. 49 percent of the students ranked teacher-led instruction as the most comfortable class setting. It is important to keep in mind that many of these students had already experienced seminars in other classes and in previous grades.

35 percent of the population valued working one on one with a teacher as the most important educational opportunity. 48 percent of the population self identified as introverted. Almost every class observed included at least one or two students who failed to contribute a single word to the seminar. Many of these failing students were repeat offenders, but some were new ones who had previously earned passing marks on seminars.

The occasional silence of students suggested that students simply have on and off days. This would mean we would need more than a handful of observations to determine whether individuals are truly acting out of personality type or learning preference. My study observed six seminars over the course of several months. The students who repeated their silence during the seminars demonstrated their introverted reflective learning style, but some also demonstrated chronic anxiety problems associated with a psychological condition, not their personality type or learning style. The stark difference between anxiety and introversion should be distinguished.

As with the students in the college study, the high school students also shared their anguish over forced dialogue in the seminars. One student explained, "I like to think about my responses so they sound organized, but by the time I'm done it's too late." Another student echoed: "I had a lot to say but I never got a chance. I also get nervous." One student explained, " I am very self-conscious...I dislike speaking when there is an opportunity that a conversation can lead to debate. This is because I detest having to defend my answer." Many students talked about how they didn't like domination of conversations and the "staged sort of feeling" that seminars have. One student argued that seminars just become a "battleground for dominance over the spotlight to speak." Several expressed how their peers, even the nicest ones, became rude out of desperation to gain points. One student even confirmed my thesis: "they [seminars] discriminate against shy people."

All of the participants, in both the college and high school studies, valued teacher-led instruction. Most said it was a necessity. Whether they academically reaped the benefits is undetermined, but it has been found that direct instruction of text structure helps improve writing, particularly with students with learning disabilities.[141] The introverted students also all argued for alternative assignments like tests, written responses, or written annotations of the assigned texts.

Like the participants in my research, students elsewhere have shared uncertain sentiments towards social learning. An associate professor of chemistry had a class that was particularly vocal in their opposition to collaborative classwork.[137] The students complained that it was hard to focus, difficult to understand the material, and that working in groups actually added to their confusion. They argued that they would rather hear an expert explain the material in class.

The value of collaborative learning is inconclusive with mixed findings.[138] There are far more studies showing problems with social constructivist methods than expected. Group discussions, like the seminar, are different from teacher-led whole class discussions because the latter has direction and defined focus. Group conversations may be confusing to some students. Evidence of learning in groups is often trivial and group work can feel superficial or rushed and does not allow time to ponder.[10]

One study by the Virginia Tech Carilion Research Institute shows that group work can actually have negative effects on aptitude by inhibiting expressions of intellect.[139] The study found that some students are actually harmed by group work.[139] As Diane Senechal pointed out, "We are surrounded by collective slogans..." which are pushed by pro social constructivist theorists who seek to silence teachers.[10]

As a result of one side's beliefs, group learning is promoted more in schools. Most instructors enjoy using group work with their students because it diversifies the teaching and learning experience, but they also know it has limits. Students see the value of group work and appreciate it in theory, but most seem to prefer individualistic assignments. Half of the college population ranked group presentations as least preferred and the other half ranked it as third. And as I know from my student surveys of the past, most students dread group work. Many of the students in my research echoed the same negative sentiment towards group learning.

Even though a seminar is not technically group learning in the way my students collaborate on research project presentations in groups of three to four, there is still a group dynamic. For example, students lead seminars, which means there are always three or four students with the same role. They do not necessarily collaborate prior to the seminar, but they essentially work together to run the student-led discussion in a large group setting. As indicated in the literature, collaborative learning only appeals to extroverts.[140] These kinds of active approaches to learning leave out introverts. But even the most extroverted students, who supposedly thrive in more active environments, also have negative opinions of group work. One of my questions was whether more social-based teaching practices in line with social constructivist methods might have an unfavorable effect on students.

Teachers may be expecting students to simply adapt. Perhaps they may be able to adapt, but the question remains to what degree can they adapt?

And who is best able to adapt?

Female or male?

Extrovert or introvert?

And if introverts, and the majority of learning styles, must adapt to a mandated teaching of extroversion, why are extroverts not expected to adapt?

My research is not meant to show a universal representation of the entire population with a diverse sampling of students; we already have those in studies from the past fifty years. My research reveals the deeper experience they have in different learning environments. But despite these factors, theorists and administrators will continue to demand that students do more talking and less listening.

9. CONCLUSIONS

I can remember as a student in graduate teacher education courses how many of us meandered our way through seminars and projects just to get through them. If we were doing that, what makes us think undergraduates and high school students are any different? Most of the participants in my studies were not entirely sure why they were discussing the texts and what they were supposed to be getting from the seminars, yet the setting seemed to provide enjoyable downtime.

As much as I enjoy them when they are good, many seminars mock the behavior seen on television talk shows. Too often the students are found to express something overly sensational for effect. Many others will parrot the same ideas and words over and over. Too many others remain quiet and confused over what they should be sharing in the class discussion. The most successful students in this setting are the loudest and most entertaining.

I fully acknowledge that classroom discussion is enjoyable and has benefits in any classroom at any level. As confirmed in the research, extroverts benefit the most by having an opportunity to share their voice in class. Introverts, however, find themselves in a foreign environment. Overall, too much discussion for any personality type can be detrimental to learning in general. I have seen the best discussions slip into madness. As both a student and a teacher, I have seen classrooms morph into the set of a talk show where members compete for ratings. That's not learning.

The English classroom is typically constructivist in nature, where students read, write, and sometimes orally present their ideas, interpretations, and arguments. But typical social constructivist theory recommends teachers do little to none of the talking most of the time. Let the students talk it out, they say. Let the teacher "facilitate," they say. However, the concern is that many students, perhaps the majority of students, may not really learn best this way. Social constructivist practices in the classroom may not provide the appropriate amount of guidance that some students need to learn. There may be too much emphasis on student dialogue and not enough on reading and writing. Social constructivist practices (e.g. small group and whole class seminars) inhibit the learning potential of introverted, reflective learners.

One social constructivist assumption is that students

only learn when they are active. The definition of active is up for debate though. Should all of the students be up running around the classroom for a class to be productive? That's fine in a physical education class, but what about students who have disabilities? For the social constructivist, speaking is somehow considered active. Why is speaking considered active while thinking, note-taking, and observation are not? There are certainly times when we are physically active, but not engaged intellectually. There are certainly plenty of examples from TV talk shows of people running off their mouths without thinking. Definitions of learning are not so simple and should not be so easily accepted.

Many of the participants in my research expressed how much they benefitted from simply listening to their peers or instructor. Many students through the years have expressed their dislike of talking in class. Some of these students may have had social or developmental issues, and some may have had disabilities, including emotional disability. But many simply had a different personality. Active learning could also be defined by reading, writing, listening, and pondering, but not according to those who worship the fictitious cone of learning. Many academicians have relied on the "cone of learning," or learning pyramid with the source attributed to Edgar Dale, even though Dale himself warned not to attach numbers to his theoretical cone, which was only meant to demonstrate differences in learning and did not reflect a proven hierarchy.

The cone, or pyramid as it is sometimes referred to, has been recreated again and again in both non-scholarly and scholarly sources with numbers that have never been verified. The argument claims that we learn more by saying and doing and gives little weight to visual observation and aural learning, the latter of which contradicts the high number of auditory learners in my classes. Researchers have more recently concluded that the "cone of experience" should "be thought of as on a continuum as opposed to in a hierarchy."[29] The misuse of the "learning cone" as a guiding light to optimal learning is an act of fraud that threatens the credibility of the social sciences.

Unless there is a sudden flood of media inquiry, I imagine theorists and believers in the social constructivist cause will continue to cite the learning cone as their source for why we should abandon direct instruction. Whether or not their influence is working is another question. Many teachers in training will face the realities of the classroom once out of their teacher-training program. Many administrators will promote direct instruction to reach higher scores for their school. Many CPR and first aid courses will continue to use some direct instruction, thankfully. Many college professors will continue to use direct instruction (and lecture) in larger content-based classes, and then direct one-on-one tutorials in smaller skills-based classes, in order to advance through their quick ten-week quarters or fifteen-week semesters.

In considering other disciplines, as we should, I have come to the big questions:

What would a drama class be without actively acting or directing?

What would a music class be without actively playing the instrument?

What would a physical education class be without physical action?

What would a technology class be without hands on work?

Surely, there is a time and a place for everything, but even those active settings need some direct teacher-led instruction, just as the core academic subjects benefit from activity. The problem is when a teacher goes too far in one philosophical direction. It is all about balance.

Hopefully, no teacher would teach in a singular way. No teacher would want to do all the talking, unless they seek life-long resentment from their students or desire a perpetual sore throat. I am not ready to give up the seminar, (especially on the rare occasion when I am under the weather), but I am skeptical of those arguments for teachers to step to the sidelines all of the time. Students benefit from talking with one another at certain stages.; however, some teachers may err to focus on only student-centered learning without recognizing those who benefit from teacher-led instruction. The problem may be that constructivist theories have dominated the sphere of teacher prep institutions while presenting themselves as the underdog.

It has been recommended that traditional lectures be front-loaded or viewed prior to class using a web-based technology in order to provide extra guidance during class time.[142] Class time can be dedicated to clearing up any questions that persist. This approach could help introverted learners. However, it should be warned that despite the excitement for his approach (especially on the web by those in the business and math areas), ironically there is no statistical evidence of the success of this trendy "flipped" classroom approach, and students-in-need may be missing out on the benefits of teacher-led instruction.

Another type of instruction called Whole Brain Instruction has made waves on the Internet with plenty of supporters and critics. This type of instruction is rapid and almost militaristic. The approach can be seen on YouTube videos and is so wild you could mistake it for a parody of teaching. The chaotic shift back and forth from a loud fast-paced teacher shouting instructions to a frenzy of student to student discussion makes this nearly impossible for a reflective introvert to succeed. The introvert does not stand a chance in this environment; they simply cease to exist. The objective of this robotically repetitious instruction is to push students to be "active" learners because the assumption is that students do not learn if they are not talking, moving, or teaching each other. Simply listening, reading, or thinking is not learning to the social constructivist, so they went to a whole new extreme with "Whole Brain" teaching. While some teachers across the nation are taking up this method and spending lots of money paying the educational consultants who created this approach, there are no scientific studies that confirm the effectiveness. All they have is someone's word. Of course, teachers can create a structured lesson on their own using direct instruction without having to go to these extremes.

One other concern is the diminishing emphasis on texts. Some scholars have argued for no textbooks, no lessons, and no worksheets in language arts classes and have advocated a class that uses conversation and games.[143] Some have argued that we should be focused on "big ideas rather than facts" but what do these "big ideas" look like?[143] But I wonder why we should value opinion over truth? Some scholars claim that students learn more about their neighborhood by investigating than they do in textbooks.[144] The huge problem here is students are not in school to learn about their neighborhoods. They go to school to learn about things other than their homes and neighborhoods. School is an escape from the bubble where you come from and a view of possibilities that your neighborhood does not always provide. Destroying the purpose of school oppresses those in most need and keeps them where they are: in their neighborhoods. The most alarming aspect of these arguments is that some scholars have argued for a change in schools of education so they could better influence teachers to teach the way they want them to teach, with games and conversations.[144]

On the other side of the spectrum, it has been recommended that content and themes should be avoided in writing classes.[145] To those who preach this approach, content and theme-based approaches leave the students with banal opinions and do not contribute to their learning how to write.[145] In this English class, a student would not use an anthology of readings, and would instead focus on learning grammar and rhetoric.[145] The strong emphasis on grammar and rhetoric itself is an old-school approach to English instruction. I would not argue, as some scholars would, that all grammar instruction should be eliminated, but I would not make it the entire course curriculum, or even a very large part of it. Remarkably, both the progressive and conservative approaches to instruction leave out the most important part of English instruction: the texts we should be reading. The learning context in my research was built entirely around my philosophy that we learn about writing by reading texts.

Another line of thought believes students should solve problems and learn by discovery.[146] The seminars used in my studies are essentially discovery in nature because the students discover themes in a reading. Seminars could also include problems to sort out. I also like to use book or web quests for effective discovery learning, where the students seek out information in the text. These quests are guided discovery learning because the teacher directs them to what specific answers they should be looking for.

There is concern about unguided discovery learning such as seminars because students are overwhelmed by stimulus. Discovery learning also violates all five cognitive principles and is an extremely "slow, ineffective way of accumulating information..."[44] My findings are supported by the argument that discovery learning and social interaction may not add up to effective learning.

Research at Portland State University suggests that building in a structured class discussion for reflection is an important part of learning.[122] However, it is still not clear how this would appeal to the more introverted students. All of my participants had a very structured environment, yet they still felt lost at times.

Carnegie Mellon Eberly Center for Teaching Excellence[147] listed the different reasons why students do not participate in class discussion. These reasons include not completing reading assignments, lack of focus, individual style of personalities, cultural values, inexperience in discussion, lack of background knowledge, and tardiness. With so many variables around why students do not participate, it would be too easy to simplify the solutions by examining only one reason on the list such as personality. The most we can do is try to improve our classroom dialogue. Should teachers discuss "how to learn" before they embark on each lesson? It might depend on how much time you have with the students.

Some educators will argue that metacognition should be up to the student. Students may very well need more time to learn how to learn, but what discipline or course will dedicate more time for this?

Math and science? Very unlikely.

In most cases, it falls on an English or Humanities course, which means less instructional time for language, research, logic, empathy, and critical thinking skills.

Technology has also been promoted as the solution to everything, but there are problems with this line of thought. I am by no means living in the stone age of teaching, though there are far greater teachers who have no need for any of my devices. I use technology to complement instruction, not substitute it. However, many theorists and tech-savvy instructional designers seem to promote substitution of instruction with technology, the way I fear those passionate about classroom dialogue are doing with discussions. The assumption is that we need to accommodate the digital natives and that technology holds all of the solutions for a better education.

Some have pointed out the drawbacks to clickers, claiming they slow down, fragment, and trivialize lessons.[10] One college student said using clickers did not compare to the details of a lecture[10] The use of clickers assumes students will learn on their own and removes the explanatory lecture leaving students on their own to struggle with material outside of class.[10] The justification for clickers is that they promote active learning and engagement, which theorists hope will replace a boring teacher at the front of a room reciting facts. The argument goes: Low student attention spans require us to accommodate these learners in whatever fashion, even if it means competing with their wild sources of entertainment. Diane Senechal reflected how strange it is today that a teacher must compete with entertainment.[10] Senechal posed the question, if students grow used to videos, games, and other computerized instruction, how will they function in the face-to-face classrooms, or even worse, how will they function in the real world environment of a workplace?[10] There may be more problems with technology than solutions, and most of the problems on the horizon are not yet getting the proper attention in the academic community.

Both teacher-led instruction and seminars are counter to the game-based, technological approach. Seminars actually get students talking to each other live in person, as opposed to through texting and social media in the already overly technological dependent world. But both methods can be corrupted by technology, since the desire for kinesthetic appeal with clickers or I-Pads can override other considerations. However, using some limited forms of technology to complement, but not replace, instruction can add to the learning experience of visual and observation learners. I would not rule out future but careful use of these technologies to complement teacher-led instruction and seminars while also appealing to visual and kinesthetic learners, but this is another area for researchers to explore.

The side of direct and explicit instruction has lost in the verbal argument, but won in practicality, as many teachers resort to traditional practices upon settling into their first jobs. The real losers though are the students, who would benefit from a hybrid of both philosophies. One study found only 'social' learners showed a strong preference for group activity. All others had a preference for didactic teaching.[136] My interviews revealed how students perceive the methods. Their opinion does seem favorable of the seminar, but they are skeptical of its learning potential or objective.

The pedagogy debates over what we ought to be teaching and how we ought to be teaching it will continue. Curricula trends ebb and flow. Skills are now often pitted against knowledge and facts, as if they cannot exist simultaneously. The debate over the formation of knowledge exists among education psychologists, theorists, and educators. This debate feeds directly into curriculum decisions and directly affects the classroom. Despite Constructivist theory dominating the field in an age of self-paced module-based math courses that seem to remove the human instructor from the forefront, all the participants in my research seemed to value the teacher-led instruction of English.

Less knowledge actually promotes less social justice, according to E.D. Hirsch who points out that promoted alternatives to the banking theory of school have failed to improve the conditions of disadvantaged students.[6] Hirsch argued: "The dichotomy between subject and child has too often resulted in failure to teach children the subjects and the skills they need."[6]

Michael Apple, who is considered at the forefront of promoting neo-Marxist ideology[43] disagrees with Hirsch. Apple fires up the perpetual debate by coming back to the knowledge tension when he argues that the core in core knowledge is not the same for everyone.[43] But following Apple's line of reasoning reduces all education to a self-paced college course in independent studies. This is a very different setting than an elementary or secondary classroom where standards ensure that students are taught common knowledge and facts. Perhaps the challenge is finding or agreeing upon what those facts should be.

Many other researchers have disputed Apple's assertion that core knowledge does not lead to academic achievement. Like Hirsch, award-winning teacher Rafe Esquith has argued how lack of background knowledge hurts poor disadvantaged students. Prior knowledge is one of the four factors that outline how well students identify. The process of obtaining this prior knowledge may be debatable, but disputing the validity of knowledge seems so counterintuitive to a liberal education. Constructivism moves away from a foundation of knowledge in education, even though epistemology still really matters.[136]

It could be said that the two extremes hold their equivalent consequences: "Totalitarian authority crushes other voices, while laissez faire egalitarianism can produce aimless talk."[134] But it does not need to be one or the other in an either/or false dichotomy. Some social constructivist theorists have argued that learning is a social process and that "students do not learn alone but rather in collaboration."[152] However, this may be a rigid definition of learning that is faulted by its false dichotomy of either learn together or do not learn at all.

There is no place for false dichotomies in academic writing.[153] There is no place for false dichotomies in academia, period. There is no reason why we cannot teach using a set of balanced tools, strategies, and activities. My personal belief is that we can improve education by being both collective and reflective.

Some have gone as far as asserting that "persistent non-participation may be a symptom of a deeper problem" and that you should see the student in your office.[74] Again, this seems to be a misunderstanding of introversion and reflective learning. Many critics would argue that education is not supposed to be like a tour, but an extroverted education for the introvert is very much like being on an expedition with an incompetent tour guide. They need a director who sets up each scene for them. Sometimes that scene will involve contributing something verbally, and sometimes that scene will involve quietly listening and thinking. We need to understand and accommodate personality types.

10. RECOMMENDATIONS

We need to respect the rights and needs of introverted students. In order to do so, we need to better understand the natural differences across students who are more or less extroverted, with differing learning styles and varying learning preferences. We should not assume the students are socially incapable of completing any of these socially-active tasks. Nor should we assume they lack the communication skills to excel at them. Many introverted students are actually very skilled presenters, performers, and speakers and do quite well in front of large audiences. The problem develops when the student has to work in groups or rely on a communal discussion of a topic. Even if they complete the task, they may do it feeling uncomfortable, and as a result the student may not be learning as much or as well as they could be.

The social constructivist approach through dialogue assumes students learn through discussion, which they would define as active. Some scholars have recommended open-ended discussion, but admit that students may need teacher correction.[99] Because there are problems with circular conversation and unsupportable lines of inquiry, a solution needs to be implemented for non-participation and superficial participation.[99]

Recommended improvements to seminars include more defined goals or listening more closely and speaking out at least once. Some recommend holding more seminars to improve seminars, but this approach fails to acknowledge learning styles or personality and never explains why some had their head down, were silent, or left early.

Some scholars have recommended dividing up learning preferences and placing one type of learner in each group,[146] which I could do with the leaders of the seminar, but this still does not consider personality type and the unnatural state of social constructivist learning for introverts. My studies had plenty of students who remained silent or conveniently avoided class altogether on the day of the seminar. Increasing the percentage of the grade attached to seminars would only have two effects: improve the performance of some students or push some students out. The latter is not worth the risk.

One new and more promising strategy for teachers is called Explicit Instruction, which is direct instruction with more teacher-student interaction where students still actively construct and process knowledge.[5] Because there are accommodations for diverse learners in Explicit Instruction[5], this research-based method may prove to be successful and may be of interest for teachers looking to adapt future lessons with these issues in mind. Choral response, signaled response, random questioning, and written responses are some of the ways to make learning more interactive during teacher-led instruction.[5]

Teachers on all levels should provide experiences in all areas of the learning cycle to accommodate all learners and increase the student's range of learning styles.[71] Since "individuals vary in their preferred learning style" pedagogy should value variety and diversity[136] Constructivist pedagogy is not effective for all learning styles and a teaching approach from one perspective does not reach all learners.[136] Even the most extroverted, independent, or social students in my studies confirmed a strong desire for guidance with teacher-led instruction.

Distance-based study is one option for students who are more introverted and reflective. Since on-line learning is independent in nature and allows much time for reflection, this may be an ideal setting, unless the online course requires live web discussions via Google Hangout or Wimba. Even the integration of these can be balanced out so students are not graded down. Online interaction has actually been shown to help introverts find their place and makes them more comfortable with interacting. Introverts tend to do well in the online environment and actually prefer computer-mediated communication. One study found that introverts actually preferred online classes and extroverts preferred face-to-face classes.[148] Future research could also be conducted to determine the auditory needs of both introverts and extroverts. With time to reflect, introverts can do quite well in online learning settings, but what about students in seated classes? Introverted students should not be pushed to enroll in all online classes.

Learning preference theory would suggest technology holds great appeal to different types of learners, especially those with visual and kinesthetic preferences. Teachers can utilize some elements of technology like e-books with built-in exercises, PowerPoint presentations, Blackboard discussion boards, and video tutorials. VoiceThread is also a wonderful online tool that enables students to post presentations and then return for responses. VoiceThread assignments for homework allow ample time for students to reflect. This approach allows reflective learners the time they need, but also give socially active learners the forum they desire, in either a seated or online environment.

Alone time is a must, with or without technology, in or out of class. Returning to Gardner's theory of Multiple Intelligences, we are reminded of society's intrapersonal needs. Interpersonal activity can be distracting, and seminars have the potential to give license to those kinds of distractions. Teachers should also not be forced into thinking they have to oblige to the wishes of theorists.

After all, we are the ones who work with the students.

Some have recommended using narrative writing and reflective journaling to increase the intrapersonal form of intelligence in all students.[141] Community service learning effectively touches on all the cycles of learning and leads to deeper learning. Perhaps the community service model holds the key. One school in London implemented strategies to better accommodate introverts: quiet rooms, an opt-out clause for group work, and a study room.[17]

Personality awareness is critical. Introverts and extroverts behave differently, while reflective and active learners learn differently. This is the one conclusion that seems to echo through my findings. Why they learn differently may depend upon biological factors. How they learn differently may be more difficult to identify. As one critic argued: "Being an introvert just means that I need time by myself to recharge my battery..."[57] We should question whether teachers are pushing students into uncomfortable and unnecessary activities, which would be counteractive in a learning environment, since introverts like to talk to one person at a time and are often uncomfortable with a group of people.[57] We must not try to turn introverts into extroverts. If anything, as John Taylor Gatto argued, educators should challenge their students "with plenty of solitude so that they can learn to enjoy their own company, to conduct inner dialogues."[49]

Recent research has demonstrated "that the less academically successful students are, the more important it is to accommodate their learning style preferences."[149] Research has also shown how knowledge of learning-style preferences increases student achievement and reduces dropout rates.[149] Learning styles can be a critical part of a student's success since they represent "each person's biologically and experientially induced characteristics that either foster or inhibit achievement."[150] People simply prefer to learn in different ways.

In regular seated classes, introverted and reflective students need a balance of instruction consisting of teacher-directed lessons that include methods such as direct instruction, integrated, inductive, and teacher-led discussions. Instructors should spend more time developing these teaching methods, and administrators should promote them through professional development opportunities. A variety of instructional methods will benefit all students and create multiple pathways to learning. Student presentations and seminars can still be a part of the equation and ideally would increase as students moved up through the levels of education.

A general core undergraduate 101 course, especially at a community college, would need to be centered around teacher-led instruction that grounds the novice student with a foundation. A graduate or professional course might naturally have a heavier reliance on student participation. Dare I say it—a high performing set of university students at the undergraduate level may also be able to participate more, regardless of their personality or learning preference. The reason for this odd difference is those students have a higher level of background knowledge at an earlier age. But none of this means all Ivy League students are extroverts— maybe they're expected to be, maybe they're shaped to be, but you can't take the introvert out of the introvert.

If any collaborative work is to be done at all in a first year community college course, it should be minimal and in small groups or pairs. The larger the group the more complicated it is. In an English course, there are ample opportunities to share your independent work, and peer review is just one option.

Another possible solution is independent work, which is quite natural in a writing course. This is where technology does play a role. Individualized instruction has been traditionally used with workbooks In developmental writing courses and journal writing and grammar worksheets in composition. Now individualized instruction can be used with e-books and software. Developmental math has already begun to take advantage of technology and many colleges now offer self-paced independent courses that are completed in modules. Technology also has many options for developmental English. For several years, I used an e-book titled *Writer's Help*, published by Bedford St. Martins, which featured assigned tutorials and interactive exercises. The students could retake the exercises as many times as they needed in order to master the skills, and the instructor has a much easier time assessing each student. The work can be completed in class for instructor guidance or for homework. Individual learning does show students learn more when mixing the type of material studied in a single setting, much the way a person works out multiple parts of the body during a gym workout.[151] If we keep this in mind, independent work could be especially useful for those who are reflective learners.

In conclusion, teachers at all levels can benefit from acknowledging learning styles and other forms of brain-based learning. While not all classes have the opportunity to administer more complex surveys like the MBTI or Kolb Learning Style Inventory, there are simpler and quicker surveys an instructor can use during the first week of classes. Pre-assessment can be an invaluable part of the learning process. Class activity that relies on heavy student participation can be better structured and students can be paired up or placed in small groups of three instead of large groups. Even simple awareness of the styles and different personalities can help instructors plan a course that appeals to a diverse student population. Instructors should resist the notion that there is anything wrong with direct teaching methods. Collaborative activities and group discussions can be used along with teacher-led instruction and individualized instruction. A balance among these approaches will lead to a better learning environment.

Epilogue: Story Tellers

Throughout my career in education, I have heard many colleagues and professors complain about the lack of student participation in class. "Why don't they talk?" "Is there something wrong with them?" "They must not be reading!" As a student I watched many professors and teachers (often introverts themselves) engage with the one or two extroverts in the room and leave everyone else in the room to be a spectator of the dialogue between teacher and "teacher's pet." I have also observed classes that pushed introverts into a mosh pit of required participation with a heavier portion of the grade, which is a subjective way of grading. No one wants a class to be silent, but do we really want a class that is all talk and no action, no reading, no reflection, no instructor guidance, and no modeling? I teach writing, not talking.

One of my greatest teachers, Professor Emeritus Ray Mariels of Portland State University, would sit at the front of the room and tell stories. His soft spoken lectures on literature seemed more like a story-telling session, and his digressions into rich and humorous metaphors were often the most insightful part of the course. Some students asked questions and added their input along the way, but we all mostly listened. I found his literature courses intellectual and funny, enlightening and light, academic and adventurous.

Surely, someone in his class along the way found it boring, just as there will always be someone in every class, no matter what you do, what tricks you have, or what dance you perform, who does not connect or refuses to open up to the subject you are teaching. Does that mean Professor Mariels should have given up his stories, so that the bored, unengaged student could be accommodated with an alternative activity, one that results in a meandering discussion of student gibberish? My education would have been so empty without a teacher like Professor Mariels.

Education theorists from the constructivist background would not have appreciated Professor Mariels' methods because they were "teacher-centered" and not "student-centered." They might say he talked too much and expected his students to absorb his knowledge. They might say his classroom was passive or unengaged. Yet I learned more in his classes than any other class.

The rich metaphors and allegories in his few classes surpass all the presentations and seminars from my entire education, in memory so many years later. The lessons from his stories continue to come to me, like the lack of permanence in life as illustrated in John Keats' "Ode on a Grecian Urn" in a recurring reminder every time I see someone eat a melting ice-cream cone, the metaphor Professor Mariels used to explain the concept.

It makes me feel bad for those theorists because they fail to understand the enormous intellect that evolves from such a class. They obviously experienced something very different in their own education. Or perhaps they simply did not appreciate the rich experience of a gifted teacher. Perhaps they resent the experience for some psychological reason. Or perhaps they just want to keep that experience all to themselves.

But the constructivist theories make me feel even worse for the gifted, charismatic teacher with wonderful stories, who is persuaded not to share their gifts with students, trained instead to sit on the sidelines as a facilitator. Early in their career, they are silenced by theorists or administrators who lack their personality and soul. Their gifts are suppressed. Their confidence for those gifts is repressed. They are told to round the students up in groups like cattle and give them games to play, puzzles to figure out, and let them talk it all out. No other threat oppresses the natural teacher more than the eradication of their ability to teach.

Even worse, my sympathy is with the many reflective learners who will miss out on a truly special education because their teachers were coerced to doubt their own intuitions. They will instead sit through hours of gibberish from their loudest most confident peers. They will wrangle with difficult dominating extroverts in group projects. Their attention span and academic focus will diminish more. Many students are now trained from an early age to expect every class to resemble a gossip circle on cable TV, so they don't even know what they're missing because they've never seen it.

However, I do not believe all teachers will give into the theoretical demands of theorists and schools of education, the same way many do not let the testing companies and state policy makers dictate how subjects should be taught. Teachers with personality and spirit will continue to tell stories, share knowledge, and teach skills directly. Maybe this approach will not be accepted by scholars, or their administrators, or their colleagues, but those who have had a Professor Mariels in their education will know it is part of their job to share with the students and direct them into the future.

Regardless of learning style, learning preference, or personality type, most of us still love to listen. A talk-show mentality has yet to change this ancient love for listening that can be traced as far back before any written language existed. Story telling will live on.

The skills of reading and writing, as well as the ability for logical thinking, are really what is most presently threatened by prejudice of personality, but the necessity for all of them remains. In addition to knowledge and analysis of great literature, an important part of Professor Mariels' job was to help students think through an analytical lens and write better academic papers. The writing assignment itself, the evolutionary result of the guidance and modeling in class, and the post assignment commentary are all part of what goes on inside the student outside the classroom, sometimes days, weeks, months, even decades later. For these extended lessons to work, a writing teacher must challenge a student, inspire and enlighten, and equip them with the skills they need to succeed. They can't do any of that if the students are too busy talking.

ABOUT THE AUTHOR

William K. Lawrence has been dedicated to the field of education for over eighteen years and has taught writing, literature, humanities, and the social sciences at numerous universities and community colleges in multiple states. He has a Doctorate in Education from Northeastern University and a Masters in Education from George Washington University, in addition to several other degrees. His previous book on education is titled *Learning and Personality*. His creative publications include poems and stories in various literary journals, a trilogy of poetry chapbooks, several collections of poetry, and the education novel *The Punk and the Professor.*

CITED REFERENCES

[1] Kolb, D. A. (1984). *Experiential learning: Experience as the source of learning and development.* Englewood Cliffs, NJ: Prentice Hall.

[2] Laney, M. O. (2002). *The introvert advantage.* New York, NY: Workman Publishers.

[3] Osborne, J. F. (1996). Beyond Constructivism. *Science Education,* 80(1). 53-82. p. 75.

[4] JilardiDamavandi, A. Mahyuddin, R. Elia, H, Daud S & Shabani, J. (2011). Academic achievement of students with different learning styles. *International Journal of Psychological Studies.* Vol. 3(2), 186-192.

[5] Goeke, J. L. (2009). *Explicit instruction: a framework for meaning direct teaching.* Upper Saddle River, NY: Merrill.

[6] Hirsch, E. D. (1996). *The schools we need and why we don't have them.* New York, NY: Doubleday.

[7] Barnard-Brak, L., Lan, W. Y., & Paton, V. (2010). Profiles in self-regulated learning in the online learning environment. *International Review of Research in Open and Distance Learning,* 11(1), 61-80.

[8] Gusentine, S. D. & Keim, M. C. (1996). The learning styles of community college art students. *Community College Review,* 24(3), 17.

[9] Cain, S. (2012). *Quiet: The power of introverts in a world that can't stop talking.* New York, NY: Crown.

[10] Senechal, D. (2012). *Republic of noise: The loss of solitude in schools and culture.* Lanham, MD: Rowman and Littlefield.

[11] Storr, A. (1988). *Solitude: A return to the self.* New York, NY: Ballantine Books.

[12] Henjum, A. (1982). Introversion: a misunderstood individual difference among students. *Education,* 103(1).

[13] Galagan, P. (2012, May). Quiet time: should extroverts learns to sit down and shut up? *T & D.* American Society for Training & Development.

[14] Zeisset, C. (2006). *The art of dialogue: Exploring personality differences for more effective communication.* Gainesville, FL: Center for Applications of Personality Type, Inc.

[15] Duman, B. (2010). The effects of brain-based learning on the academic achievement of students with different learning styles. *Educational Sciences: Theory & Practice,* 10(4), 2077.

[16] Helgoe, L. (2008). *Introvert power: Why your inner life is your hidden strength.* Naperville, IL: Source Books.

[17] Pennington, B. T. (2012). *Educating the introverted child: The silent cohort.* Lexington, KY: Independent.

[18] Nussbaum, M. E. (2002). How introverts versus extroverts approach small-group argumentative discussions. *The Elementary School Journal,* 102(3), 183-197. doi:10.1086/499699

[19] Dembling, S. (2012). *The introvert's way.* New York, NY: Perigee.

[20] Cremin, L. A. (1976). *Public education,* New York, NY: Basic Books.

[21] Davidson, T. (1970). *A history of education.* New York, NY: Ams Press.

[22] Lattuca, L. (2006). The constructivist we're looking for. *Journalism and Mass Communication Educator*, 60(4).

[23] Duffy, T., & Cunningham D. (1996). Constructivism: Implications for the design and delivery of instruction. In Jonassen, D. H. (Ed.), *Handbook of Research for Educational Communications and Technology*, New York: Simon and Schuster, 170-198.

[24] Hirsch, E. D. (2009). *The making of Americans: Democracy and our schools.* New Haven, CT: Yale University Press.

[25] Robinson, K. (2010). Changing education paradigms, TED Ideas Worth Spreading. Retrieved at June 14, 2011, from the website Temoa: Open Educational Resources (OER) Portal at http://www.temoa.info/node/51092

[26] Peters, L., Shmerling, S., & Karren, R. (2011). Constructivist pedagogy in asynchronous online education: Examining proactive behavior and the impact on student engagement levels. *International Journal on E-Learning*, 10(3): 311-330.

[27] Thalheimer, W. (2006). People remember 10%, 20%...Oh really? *Will at Work Learning*. Retrieved from: www.willatworklearning.com

[28] Dwyer, F. (2010). Edgar Dale's cone of experience: A quasi-experimental analysis. *International Journal Of Instructional Media*, 37(4), 431-437.

[29] Lalley, J. P., & Miller, R. H. (2007). The learning pyramid: Does it point teachers in the right directions? *Education*, 128(1), 64-79.

[30] Pattison, R. (1987). *The triumph of vulgarity.* New York, NY: Oxford University Press.

[31] Gleason, M. M. (1995). Using direct instruction to integrate reading and writing for students with learning disabilities. *Reading and Writing Quarterly*, 11(1). 91.

[32] Zeisset, C. (2006). *The art of dialogue: Exploring personality differences for more effective communication.* Gainesville, FL: Center for Applications of Personality Type, Inc.

[33] Hirsch, E. D. (2006). *The knowledge deficit: Closing the shocking education gap for American children.* New York, NY: Houghton Mifflin.

[34] Kozol, J. (2005). *The shame of the nation.* New York, NY: Three Rivers Press.

[35] Gallagher, K. (2009). *Readicide: How schools are killing reading and what you can do about it.* Portland, ME: Stenhouse Publishers.

[36] Weissmann, J. (2014). The decline of the American book lover. *The Atlantic.* Retrieved from www.theatlantic.com

[37] Prince, M. B. (2007). A new beginning in college writing. *Journal of Education*, 188(3), 1-27.

[38] Pattison, R. (1982). *On literacy: The politics of the word from Homer to the age of rock.* New York, NY: Oxford University Press.

[39] Clark, R. E., Yates, K., Early, S., & Moulton, K. (2009). An analysis of the failure of electronic media and discovery-based learning: Evidence for the performance benefits of guided training methods. In K. H. Silbert & R. Foshay (Eds.) *Handbook of training and improving workplace performance,* Volume I: Instructional design and training delivery. (pp. 263-297). New York: John Wiley and Sons.

[40] Adler, M. J. (1982). *The Paideia proposal: An educational manifesto.* NY: Simon & Schuster.

[41] Rushkoff, D. (2013). *Present shock: When everything happens now.* New York, NY: Current.

[42] Cherwin, K. A. (2013). The advantages of not multi-tasking. *HigherEd Jobs.* Retrieved from www.higheredjobs.com

[43] Cuozzo, C. (2005). *The process of disciplines.* Arlington, VA: Authorhouse.

[44] Sweller, J. (2009). What human cognition architecture tells us about Constructivism. In S. Tobias & T. M. Duffy (Eds), *Constructivist instruction: Success or failure?* (pp. 127-143). New York, NY: Routledge.

[45] Andrews, T. M., Leonard, M. J., Colgrove, C. A., & Kalinowski, S. T. (2011). Active learning not associated with student learning in a random sample of college biology courses. CBE. *Life Sciences Education.*10, p. 394-405.

[46] Kirscher, P. A., Sweller, J., and Clark, R. E. (2006). Why minimal guidance during instruction does not work: an analysis of the failure of constructivist, discovery, problem-based, experiential, and inquiry-based teaching. *Educational Psychologist*, 41 (2), 75-86.

[47] Jung, C. (1921). *Psychological types.* Princeton, NJ: Princeton University Press. 1975 reprint.

[48] Goleman, D. (1995). *Emotional intelligence: Why it can matter more than IQ.* New York, NY: Bantam.

[49] Gatto, J. T. (2009). *Weapons of mass instruction.* Gabriola Island, British Columbia, New Society Publishers.

[50] Kagan, J. (1994). *Galen's prophecy: Temperament in human nature.* New York, NY: Basic Books.

[51] Callero, P. (2009). *The myth of individualism.* Lanham, MD: Rowan and Littlefield.

[52] Stop Bullying. (2013). *Effects of bullying.* U.S. Department of Health & Human Services. 200 Independence Avenue, S.W. Washington, D.C. 20201. Retrieved from stopbullying.gov

[53] Tani, F., Greenman, P. S., Schneider, B. H., & Fregoso, M. (2003). Bullying and the Big Five. *School Psychology International,* 24(2), 131.

[54] Martin, J. N. & Nakayama, T. K. (2011). *Experiencing intercultural communications.* 4th ed. NY, NY: McGraw Hill.

[55] Emerson, R.W. (1841). "Self-Reliance." *Essays.*

[56] Cain, S. (2013, May). Two-minute Interview. *NEA Higher Education Advocate,* 30(3).

[57] Morris, J. C. (1994). Introverts. *Young Children,* 49(2). 32-33.

[58] Aron, E. N. (1999). High sensitivity as one source of fearfulness and shyness: Preliminary research and clinical implications. In L. A. Schmidt & J. Schulkin (Eds.), *Extreme fear, shyness, and social phobia: Origins, biological mechanisms, and clinical outcomes* (pp. 251-272). New York: Oxford University Press.

[59] Aron, E. N. (1997). *The highly sensitive person: How to thrive when the world overwhelms you.* Secaucus, NJ: Birch Lane Press.

[60] Humane Society of the United States. (2011). *U.S. pet ownership statistics.* Retrieved at:
www.humanesociety.org

[61] Myers-Briggs, I. & Myers, P. B. (1980). *Gifts differing: Understanding personality type.* Mountain View, CA: CPP.

[62] Williams, D. (2004). *Sin boldly: Dr. Dave's guide to writing the college paper.* New York, NY: Basic Books.

[63] Silver, H. F., Strong, R. W., & Perini, M. J. (2000). *So each may learn: Integrating learning styles and multiple intelligences.* Alexandria, VA: ASCD.

[64] Jones, C., Reichard, C., & Mokhtari, K. (2003). Are students' learning styles discipline specific? *Community College Journal of Research & Practice,* 27(5), 363.

[65] Gogus, A., & Gunes, H. (2011). Learning styles and effective learning habits of university students: A case from Turkey. *College Student Journal,* 45(3), 586-600.

[66] Kolb, D. A. (1985). *Learning style inventory.* Revised edition. Boston, MA: Hay Group Resources Direct.

[67] Little, L. (2004, August). Kolb's learning styles for leaders. *Administrator,* 23(8), 8.

[68] Kolb, A. Y. & Kolb, D. A. (2005). *The Kolb learning style inventory—version 3.1 2005 technical specifications.* Boston, MA: Hay Group Resources Direct.

[69] Margerison, C. J. & Lewis, R. G. (1979). *How Work Preferences Relate to Learning Styles.* Bedfordshire, England: Management and Organisation, Development Research Center, Cranfield School of Management.

[70] Ally, M. (2004). Foundations for educational theory for online learning. *Theory and practice of online learning.* Chapter 1. Canada: Au Press.

[71] Chapman, C. & Gregory, G. H. (2002). *Differentiated instructional strategies: One size doesn't fit all.* Thousand Oaks, CA: Corwin Press.

[72] Nilson, L. B. (2003). *Teaching at its best,* 2nd ed. Bolton, MA: Anker.

[73] Wirz, D. (2004). Students' learning styles vs. professors' teaching styles. *Inquiry,* 9 (1).

[74] Felder, R. M. (1993). Reaching the second tier: Learning and teaching styles in college science education. *Journal of College Science Teaching,* 23(5), 286-290.

[75] Al-Shammari, Z., Al-Sharoufi, H., & Yawkey, T. D. (2008). The effectiveness of direct instruction in teaching English in elementary public education schools in Kuwait: A research case study. *Education,* 129, 80-90.

[76] Ally, M. & Fahy, P. (2002, August). Using students' learning styles to provide support in distance education. *Proceedings of the eighteenth annual conference on distance teaching and learning,* Madison, WI.

[77] Williams, R. A. (2001, August). *Learning styles and achievement motivation of community college students.* Dissertation Abstracts International Section A, 62.

[78] Philbin, M., Meier, E., Huffman, S., & Boverie, P. (1995). A survey of gender and learning styles. *Sex Roles: A Journal of Research,* 32(7-8), 485-495

[79] Gusentine, S. D. & Keim, M. C. (1996). The learning styles of community college art students. *Community College Review,* 24(3), 17.

[80] Tumkaya, S. (2012). The investigation of the epistemological beliefs of university students according to gender, grade, fields of study, academic success and their learning styles. *Educational Sciences: Theory & Practice, 12*(1), 88-95.

[81] Ouyang, H. (2003). Resistance to the communicative method of language instruction within a progressive Chinese university. In Anderson-Levitt, K. (Ed.) *Local meanings, global schooling: Anthropology and world culture theory.* New York, NY: Palgrave Macmillan.

[82] Chang, L. L. (1999). Sociocultural adjustment of Chinese-American students. In C. C. Park & M. M. Chi (Eds). *Asian-American Education: prospects and challenges* (pp. 1-17). Westport, CT: Bergin and Garvey.

[83] Litton, E. F. (1999). Learning in America: The Filipinio-American sociological perspective. In C. C. Park & M. M. Chi (Eds). *Asian-American Education: prospects and challenges.* Westport, CT: Bergin and Garvey.

[84] Chuong, C. H. (1999). Vietnames-American students: Between the pressure to succeed and the pressure to change. In C. C. Park & M. M. Chi (Eds). *Asian-American Education: prospects and challenges.* Westport, CT: Bergin and Garvey.

[85] Park, C. C. (1999). Schooling for Korean-American students: a sociological. In C. C. Park & M. M. Chi (Eds). *Asian-American Education: prospects and challenges.* Westport, CT: Bergin and Garvey.

[86] Nishida T. Y. (1999). Meeting the educational and sociological needs of Japanese students in American schools. In C. C. Park & M. M. Chi (Eds). *Asian-American Education: prospects and challenges.* Westport, CT: Bergin and Garvey.

[87] Venugopalan, M. (2000). *The relationship between extroversion/introversion and university- level ESL language proficiency.* University of Kansas). *ProQuest Dissertations and Theses,* 127-127 p. (250029073).

[88] Martin, J. N. & Nakayama, T. K. (2011). *Experiencing intercultural communications.* 4th ed. New York, NY: McGraw Hill.

[89] Kail, H. and Trimbur, J. (1997). *Collaborative writing,* 2nd ed. Blair Resources for Teaching writing. Upper Saddle River, NJ: Prentice Hall.

[90] Sego, A. (2003) Testing and grading. Greives, D. Ed. *Handbook II: Advanced teaching strategies,* 2003. Ann Arbor, MI: The Adjunct Advocate.

[91] Woolfolk, A. (2007). *Educational Psychology,* 10th ed. New York, NY: Pearson.

[92] Ruey, S. (2010). A case study of Constructivist instructional strategies for adult online learning. *British Journal of Educational Technology,* 41(5), 706-720.

[93] Ankerson, K. & Pable, J. (2008). *Interior design: Practical strategies for teaching and learning.* NY, NY: Fairchild.

[94] Shirley, L. J. (1998). *Pocket guide to multiple intelligences.* Clemson, SC: National Dropout Prevention Center, Clemson University.

[95] Middlecamp, C. (1997). Students speak out about collaborative work. *Teaching Stories.* Wisconsin Center for Education Research.

[96] Marzano, R. J. (2007). *The art and science of teaching.* Alexandria, VA: ASCD.

[97] Burke, J. (2010). *What's the big idea? Question-driven units to motivate reading, writing, and thinking.* Portsmouth, NH: Heinemann.

[98] Roberts, T. & Billings, C. (2012). *Teaching critical thinking.* Larchmont, NY: Eye on Education.

[99] Hale, M. S. & City, E. A. (2006). *Leading student-centered discussions: Talking about texts in the classroom.* Thousand Oaks, CA: Corwin Press.

[100] Slavin, R. E. (2008). *Educational psychology: Theory and practice,* 9th ed. New York, NY: Allyn & Bacon.

[101] Beach, R. & Myers, J. (2001). *Inquiry based English instruction: Engaging students in life and literature.* New York, NY: Teacher's College Press.

[102] Kirscher, P. A., Sweller, J., and Clark, R. E. (2006). Why minimal guidance during instruction does not work: an analysis of the failure of constructivist, discovery, problem-based, experiential, and inquiry-based teaching. *Educational Psychologist,* 41 (2), 75-86.

[103] Becker, W. C. & Gersten, R. (2001). Follow-up of Follow Through: The later effects of the direct instruction model on children in fifth and sixth grades. *Journal of Direct Instruction,* 1(1), 57-71.

[104] Armstrong, T. (2000). *Multiple intelligence in the classroom.* Alexandria, VA: Association for Supervision & Curriculum (ASCD).

[105] Gardner, H. & Walters, J. (1995). The development and education of intelligence. In R. Fogarty & J. Bellanca, (Eds.), *Multiple intelligences: A collection.* Arlington Heights, IL: IRI/Skylight Training.

[106] Fagella, K. & Horowitz, J. (1990, Sept). Different child, different style. *Instructor,* 100(2), 49-54.

[107] Gardner, H. (1995). An interview with Howard Gardner by R.J. Kirschenbaum. In R. Fogarty & J. Bellanca, (Eds.), *Multiple intelligences: A collection.* Arlington Heights, IL: IRI/ Skylight Training.

[108] Smagorinsky, P. (2007). Vygotsky and the social dynamics of classrooms. *The English Journal,* 97(2), 61-66.

[109] Nolan, J. (2003). Multiple intelligences in the classroom. *Education,* 124(1), 115-19.

[110] Margerison, C. J. & Lewis, R. G. (1979). How Work Preferences Relate to Learning Styles. Bedfordshire, England: Management and Organisation, Development Research Center, Cranfield School of Management.

[111] Hollingsworth, J. and Ybarra, S. E. (2009). Explicit direct instruction (EDI): *The power of the well-crafted, well-taught lesson.* Thousand Oaks, CA: Corwin Press.

[112] Carnine, D. W., Silbert, J., Kame'enui, E. J., & Tarver, S. G. (Eds.). (2004). *Direct Reading Instruction* (4th ed.). Upper Saddle River, NJ: Pearson.

[113] Klahr, D., Nigam, M. (2004) The equivalence of learning paths in early science instruction: Effects of direct instruction and discover learning. *Psychological Science,* 15, 661-667.

[114] Jonassen, D. (2009). Reconciling a human cognitive architecture. In S. Tobias & T. M. Duffy (Eds), *Constructivist instruction: Success or failure?* (pp. 13-33). New York, NY: Routledge.

[115] Rosenshine, B. (2009). The empirical support for direct instruction. In S. Tobias & T. M. Duffy (Eds), *Constructivist instruction: Success or failure?* (pp. 201-220). New York, NY: Routledge.

[116] National Institute for Direct Instruction, (2013). "What is Direct Instruction?" Retrieved from: www.nifdi.org

[117] Reagan, R. (2008). Direct instruction in skillful thinking in fifth-grade American history. *The Social Studies*, 99, (5), 217.

[118] The Baltimore Curriculum Project. (2009). Direct instruction. Retrieved from http://www.baltimorecp.org

[119] Addison, K., & Yakimowski, M. (2003). *An evaluation of the direct instruction program: A report prepared for the board of school commissioners.* Division of Research, Evaluation, Assessment, and Accountability, Baltimore City Public School System.

[120] Slavin, R. E., & Cheung, A. (2003). *Effective programs for English language learners: A best-evidence synthesis.* Baltimore: Johns Hopkins University.

[121] Schug, M. C., Tarver, S. G., & Western, R. D. (2001, March). Direct instruction and the teaching of early reading: A teacher-led insurgency. *Wisconsin Policy Research Institute Report*, 14 (2). Retrieved from:
http://www.wpri.org/Reports/Volume14/Vol14no2.pdf

[122] Hatcher, J. A. & Bringle, R. G. (1997). Reflection. *College Teaching*, 45(4), 153-159.

[123] Brown, A. L., & Campione, J. C. (1994). Guided discovery in a community of learners. In K. McGilly (Ed.), *Classroom lessons: Integrating cognitive theory and classroom practice* (pp.229-270). Cambridge,MA: MIT Press/ Bradford Books.

[124] Hardiman, P., Pollatsek, A., & Weil, A. (1986). Learning to understand the balance beam. *Cognition and Instruction*, 3.

[125] Thornton, P. B. (2013, May). The three D's. Thriving in academe. *NEA Higher Education Advocate*, 30(3).

[126] Esquith, R. (2003). *There are no shortcuts*. New York, NY: Pantheon.

[127] Walton, J. D. (2011). Dissonance in the critical classroom: The role of social psychological processes in learner resistance. *College Student Journal*, 45(4), 769-785.

[128] Mayer, R. E. (2009). Constructivism as a theory of learning versus constructivism as a prescription for instruction. In S. Tobias & T. M. Duffy (Eds), *Constructivist instruction: Success or failure?* (pp. 184-200). New York, NY: Routledge.

[129] Alexander, R. R. (1983). Teacher as Shaman: An educational criticism. *Studies In Art Education*, 25(1), 48.

[130] Dunn, R., Beaudry, J. S., & Klavas, A. (1989). Survey of research on learning styles. *Educational Leadership*, 46(6), 50.

[131] Brown, B. L. (1998). Learning styles and vocational education practice. Practice application brief. *Center on Education and Training for Employment*, College of Education, Ohio State University. Retrieved from http://www.calpro-online.org/eric/docs/pab00007.pdf

[132] Zapalska, A. & Brozik, D. (2006). Learning styles and online education. *Campus-wide Information Systems*, 23(6) 325-335.

[133] Chabris, C. & Simons, D. (2010). *The invisible gorilla: How our intuitions deceive us*. New York, NY: MJF Books.

[134] Baker, A. C., Jensen, P. J. & Kolb, D. A. (2002). *Conversational learning: An experiential approach to knowledge creation.* Westport, CT: Quorum.

[135] Mayer, S. J. (2012). *Classroom discourse and democracy: Making meanings together.* New York, NY: Peter Lang.

[136] Osborne, J. F. (1996). Beyond Constructivism. *Science Education*, 80(1). 53-82.

[137] Taylor, A. (2011). Top 10 reasons students dislike working in groups ... and why I do it anyway. *Biochemistry and Molecular Biology Education*, 39 (2), 219-220.

[138] Sweller, J., Ayres, P., & Kalyuga, S. (2011). *Cognitive load theory.* New York, NY: Springer.

[139] Higgins, J. (2012). Group projects yield less work. *Collegiate Times*, 37.

[140] DeLeon, L. & Jerri, K. (2000). Comparing Modes of Delivery: Classroom and On-Line (And Other) Learning. *Journal of Public Affairs Education*. 6(1), 5-18.

[141] Gleason, M. M. (1995). Using direct instruction to integrate reading and writing for students with learning disabilities. *Reading and Writing Quarterly*, 11(1). 91.

[142] Chilton, M. A. & Gurung, A. (2008). Management of lecture time: Using the web to manipulate extrinsic cognitive load. *Journal of Web-based Learning and Teaching Technologies*, 3(2).

[143] Gould, J. S. (1996) Perspectives on teaching and learning in the language arts. In C.T. Fosnot (Ed.), *Constructivism: Theory, perspectives and practice.* New York, NY: Teacher's College Press.

[144] Fosnot, C. T. (1996). *Constructivism: Theory, perspectives and practice.* New York, NY: Teacher's College Press.

[145] Fish, S. (2008). *Save the world on your own time.* New York, NY: Oxford University Press.

[146] Lincoln, F. & Rademacher, B. (2006). Learning styles of ESL students in community colleges, *Community College Journal of Research and Practice*, 30:5-6, 485-500.

[147] Center for Teaching Excellence. (2013). Students don't participate in discussions. *Enhancing Education.* Carnegie Mellon. Retrieved at: hwww.cmu.edu

[148] Harrington R. and Loffredo, D. A. (2010). MBTI personality type and other factors that relate to preference for online versus face-to-face instruction. *Internet and Higher Education*, 13, 89-95.

[149] Yeganeh, B. & Kolb, D. (2009). Mindfulness and experiential learning. *OD Practitioner*, 41(3), 13.

[150] Dunn, R. (1984). Learning Style: State of the Science. *Theory Into Practice*, 23(1), 10.

[151] Carey, B. (2010). Forget what you know about good study habits. *The New York Times. Views.* Retrieved at www.nytimes.com

[152] Zins, J. E., Bloodworth, M. R., Weissberg, R. P., & Wahlberg, H. J. (2007). The scientific base linking social and emotional learning to school success. *Journal of Educational and Psychological Consultation*, 17(2 & 3).

[153] Rubin, H. J. & Rubin, I. S. (2012). *Qualitative interviewing: The art of hearing data.* 3rd. ed. Thousand Oaks, CA: SAGE.

INDEX

Apple, Michael, 103

Asian American, 43-50

Auditory learners, 19, 36, 42, 53, 73-75, 77-79, 94

Buffet, Warren, 24

Burke, Jim, 54, 68, 71

Cain, Susan, 11, 12, 24, 29, 33, 34

Callero, Peter, 26

Carnegie Mellon, 98

Clickers, 21, 40, 100-101

Collaborative learning, 1, 2, 8, 3, 22, 51, 52, 59, 61, 62, 84, 88, 89, 112, 113

Cone of Learning, 16, 17, 18, 20, 61, 93

Constructivist, 1, 7-9, 13, 15, 16, 22, 47, 52, 55-57, 59, 65, 71, 72, 79, 80, 82, 85, 88, 89, 90, 92, 93-96, 102, 104, 106-108, 115, 116

Community College, 5, 34, 42, 70, 111, 112, 118

Cremin, Lawrence, 14

Dale, Edgar, 16, 17, 19, 93

Dembling, Sofia, 13, 43

Direct instruction, 5, 7, 10, 16, 19, 31, 39, 40, 41, 56, 60, 62-72, 85, 94, 95, 97, 99, 102, 107, 111, 113

Discrimination, 9, 40, 51

Discovery learning, 20, 98, 99

Discussion Based Learning, 1, 2, 8, 13, 40, 41, 46, 52, 54, 79, 82, 83, 86, 88, 89, 91, 92, 96, 99, 100, 106, 107, 108, 111, 113, 115

Eliot, T.S., 24

English, teaching of and methods, 2, 7, 8, 20, 55, 64, 69, 80, 81, 85, 92, 98, 103, 112, 116

Esquith, Rafe, 70, 103

First year students, 66, 112

Fleming, Neil, 36

Freud, Sigmund, 26

Gardner, Howard, 11-12, 20

Gandhi, 24

Gates, Bill, 24

Gatto, John Taylor, 26, 110

Gender, 40-41

Gore, Al, 24

Gregorc, Anthony, 35-36

Group Learning, 21, 23, 26-28, 30, 34, 53-58, 66, 69, 71, 74-86, 96-103

Helgoe, Laurie, 24

Hirsch, E.D., 16, 19, 20, 56, 57, 103

Individualized learning and instruction, 20, 31, 102-103

Inquiry based instruction, 22, 56, 72

Interpersonal, 6, 7, 11, 12, 16, 19, 42, 52, 58, 59, 63, 109

Intrapersonal, 6, 7, 34, 42, 57, 58, 60, 62, 109, 110

i-pad, 99

Jung, Carl, 23, 24, 30, 31, 35, 37, 59

Keats, John, 115

Kolb, David, 31, 41, 62

Kozol, Jonathan, 19

Kinesthetic learners, 10, 36, 42, 57, 62, 73, 74, 76-79, 101, 102, 109

Knowledge, 5, 112, 115, 116

Lazarus, Emma, 53

Learning Preferences, 4, 18, 19, 54, 63, 73, 79, 86, 106

Learning Styles, 2, 9, 11, 35-42, 49, 54, 57, 58, 90, 106-108, 110, 113

Lincoln, Abraham, 24

Multiple Intelligences, 35, 37, 57, 109

Mariels, Ray, 114-117

Myers-Briggs, 31, 35

National Institute of Direct Instruction, 69

Nilson, Linda, 52-53, 63

Online Learning, 25, 48, 98-100, 103

Oregon, 45, 68, 99

Parks, Rosa, 24

Pattison, Robert, 18, 20

Personality Types, 2, 9, 11, 30, 31, 34, 35, 37, 41, 52, 54, 58, 59, 63, 73, 76, 78, 81, 87, 92, 105, 107, 116

Portland State University, 99

Quiet, (see Susan Cain)

Roosevelt, Eleanor, 24

Rosenshine, Barack, 67

Senechal, Diane, 63, 88, 101

Socratic Method, 2, 53

Storr, Anthony, 11, 27, 31, 59

Streisand, Barbara, 24

Sweller, John, 22, 23, 56, 87, 89

Talking in education, 2, 7, 27, 31, 60-67, 71, 75, 81, 87-88, 91, 93, 99

Teacher-Led Instruction, 2-4, 35-95, 99, 101, 103-104

Technology, 29, 31, 94, 98-99, 111

VARK, 36, 77, 79

Visual learners, 40, 71, 74

VoiceThread, 109

Wholebrain Teaching, 96-97

Wozniak, Steve, 34

Writer's Help, 111

www.ingramcontent.com/pod-product-compliance
Lightning Source LLC
Chambersburg PA
CBHW031136090426
42738CB00008B/1102